Praise for *Small Business, Big Vision*

"I've never considered myself an entrepreneur. I'm a nerd and always have been, but I believe very much in the message of *Small Business, Big Vision*. I think having a vision is what's made Craigslist so successful, and I'm applying the same principle to my new initiative Craigconnects. Entrepreneurs would do well to read this book and absorb its message. The stuff that works best is driven by passion rather than dollars."

—Craig Newmark,
Founder of Craigslist

"Traveling around the country speaking to young entrepreneurs, I often get asked which business books are most helpful. I'm adding *Small Business, Big Vision* to my list! This book contains some superb insights on everything from start-up through giving back as a social entrepreneur. There is not a business owner, or business-owner-to-be who won't benefit from reading this book."

—Michael Simmons,
Co-Founder & CEO,
Extreme Entrepreneurship Tour

"If you're an entrepreneur you're going to experience the highs and lows of business, and without a big vision it's too easy to throw in the towel. Adam and Mathew's book gives you the driving force and multiple examples for creating that big vision to keep you moving forward."

—Yanik Silver,
InternetLifestyle.com

"*Small Business, Big Vision* is no pie in the sky theory but the nuts and bolts practical information that every entrepreneur needs to succeed in the dog eat dog world of starting and growing a profitable business. Get it. Study it. Apply it!"

—Chris Widener,
Author of the *Art of Influence*
and *Leadership Rules*

"So many business books are based on one guy telling you how to do it their way— what they are really saying is 'I'm awesome, so do what I did,' but this book doesn't do that. There is no blueprint to creating a successful business and mistakes are not only inevitable but even beneficial in the long term. This book doesn't do the high and mighty bit, but is a great guide to helping you get what you want . . . pour yourself a large, strong drink and enjoy."

—Calvin Ayre,
Founder of Bodog.com

"A well-written, accessible guide to help entrepreneurs dream big—even in the earliest stages of their venture."

—Jeffrey J. Bussgang,
Flybridge Capital Partners

"The principles presented in *Small Business, Big Vision* are valuable in and of themselves, and they are delivered in an easy-to-understand, direct format that helps the reader fully absorb the information so he or she can implement it in their business right away. Rarely does a book come along that covers so many important topics and does it so well. *Small Business, Big Vision* delivers!"

—Harry Chemko,
CEO, ElasticPath

small business,

BIG
VISION

small business, BIG VISION

Lessons *on* How *to* Dominate Your Market

from Self-Made Entrepreneurs

Who Did It Right

ADAM TOREN
MATTHEW TOREN

WILEY

John Wiley & Sons, Inc.

For general information on our other products and services or for technical support, please contact our Customer Care Department within the United States at (800) 762-2974, outside the United States at (317) 572-3993 or fax (317) 572-4002.

Wiley also publishes its books in a variety of electronic formats. Some content that appears in print may not be available in electronic books. For more information about Wiley products, visit our web site at www.wiley.com.

Library of Congress Cataloging-in-Publication Data:

Toren, Adam, 1975–
  Small business, big vision: lessons on how to dominate your market from self-made entreprenuers who did it right/Matthew Toren, Adam Toren.
    p. cm.
  ISBN: 978-1-118-01820-0 (pbk.)
  ISBN: 978-1-118-09858-5 (ebk)
  ISBN: 978-1-118-09859-2 (ebk)
  ISBN: 978-1-118-09860-8 (ebk)
  1. Small business–Management. 2. Entrepreneurship. 3. Success in business. I. Toren, Matthew. II. Title.
  HD62.7.T667 2011
  658.02'208—dc22

2011010999

Printed in the United States of America

10 9 8 7 6 5 4 3 2 1

Contents

Foreword

As a close friend of both Adam and Matthew Toren for many years, I was honored when they asked me to write this foreword. It wasn't so much because this is the first time that I have been formally published, but more importantly because of the compelling and exclusive content they've placed within these pages.

My hope is that this book equips you with the tools, framework, and inspiration to change the world. It is written in a straightforward, succinct, and practical format that provides the flexibility that you as a business owner need to implement actions right away toward some of your most pressing challenges.

Even more impressive is the fact that this is the first ever book that takes a case-based approach to entrepreneurship—written by, for, and with insights from some of the most successful entrepreneurs in the world. As you read on, get ready for a journey that will change the way you do business right now—not tomorrow, in a month, or in a year, but immediately.

I have earned my entrepreneurial stripes over the preceding 15 years. I started my first company at the age of 12 because my parents didn't have enough money to buy me football cleats. Since then, I have founded, built, and scaled 10 companies that have touched thousands upon thousands of people around the world, spanning from consumer products and retail, to digital media and print. I come from the school of hard knocks; nothing was ever given to me on a silver platter, and for that I feel extremely fortunate.

One of my successes has been New York Entrepreneur Week (NYEW), the third largest entrepreneur week in the world. I built it in just two years, in the face of unimaginable and daunting odds—from the economic recovery to risking my entire life savings on an idea that my friends and family thought was unfathomable. So why did I do it? Because I was passionate, and knew that my vision would make the world a better place as a result. What did I learn? There's no free lunch. Who did I meet? Adam and Matthew Toren, two of the most knowledgeable, generous, and humble entrepreneurs I have ever encountered throughout the course of my career.

Adam and Matthew are friends first and businesspeople second. That is important to mention because they didn't write this book to make money. I kid you not. They are not professional speakers, self-promoters, or marketing gurus. Instead, they are two brothers who've taken a similar path to mine and they feel a responsibility to you—a passion for giving back to those who seek to build their own entrepreneurial legacy.

In terms of gentlemen who believe in entrepreneurship as the fundamental underpinning of economies around the world, you will not find three more dedicated entrepreneurs than Adam, Matthew, and me. All three of us are extremely passionate about educational reform and entrepreneurship-based curriculum in schools around the country. Adam and Matthew previously wrote a children's book entitled *Kidpreneurs*, which is becoming widely adopted and was personally praised by President Barack Obama. I have founded the Relentless Foundation, which works in tandem with Adam and Matthew and is a 501(c)(3) nonprofit, seeking to integrate entrepreneurship into every K–12 classroom by the year 2030. I tell you the above not to self-promote, but as an example of how much the authors of this book care about you. It might sound superfluous, as you're simply reading words on a page. But guess what? If you don't believe me, e-mail us. I challenge you to do so. I guarantee that one of the three of us will personally respond to you and will help in any way, shape, or form that we can. Why? Because all three of us feel fortunate to be where we are—being able to provide our lens on the world (alongside a few of our counterparts) to you in a concise, impactful, and important book.

What Adam and Matthew have detailed in this book creates possibility for you. It provides a platform of real-world, cutting-edge insight and knowledge that will guide you toward making intelligent business decisions. The world is your oyster; it's just a matter of whether you make a pearl or a few specks of dirt out of it. Don't make the mistake of thinking that this book is the end-all be-all; instead, pull out your highlighter and sticky notes, and absorb every single nugget of advice that is provided throughout. With this book in hand, the possibilities for you and for your company are endless.

Small Business, Big Vision provides a framework for you to unleash your driven and relentless passion to achieve unprecedented growth, both personally and professionally—no matter what stage of the entrepreneurial journey you're at. From planning, to social responsibility, to marketing, this book runs the gamut in terms of critical business insights, which few people have sought to explore via an in-depth and methodical approach. This book takes you through the experiences of some of the best, brightest, and most renowned entrepreneurs in the world. Anything you've ever wondered about your entrepreneurial journey is covered, both through the insightful profiles and the authors' spot-on advice.

Being an entrepreneur is not, nor will it ever be, easy. *Small Business, Big Vision* gives you straightforward, practical advice and case studies to overcome your most pressing business challenges. What this book contains is not for the faint of heart; it is real advice from successful and well-known entrepreneurs who have done the impossible time and time again. They have defied the odds, as 95 percent of businesses fail within five years. That is the sad reality of most entrepreneurial journeys, because most business owners lack cross-vertical operating experience. *Small Business, Big Vision* provides you with the frameworks to accelerate your company's success, whether you're in the early stages of your vision or in full execution.

Over the course of my career, I have sat on boards of Fortune 100 companies, advised presidents, and negotiated deals from seed investments through those involving millions of dollars. I know what patterns to look for in entrepreneurs who have the prospect for success. *Small Business, Big Vision* provides the fundamental underpinning for your journey, as it encourages you to learn from entrepreneurs of varying backgrounds and businesses. However, they all have one important quality in common: they've lived through the struggles, catapulted themselves above the status quo, and breathed deep the sweet smell of success. Very simply, the entrepreneurs profiled in this book encompass the number-one ethos dictating entrepreneurial success: being willing to stop at nothing to achieve everything.

Take a second and ask yourself: Do you *really* know what you want out of life? Do you have an understanding of your personal and professional objectives? Get clear about what you want by taking a few minutes now to stop and think. The reality of entrepreneurship is much different than the glorified tales you see on TV or in the news. In actuality, being an entrepreneur is going to be the hardest test of your life—mentally, physically, and emotionally. You can read just about any blog or research paper, and it will provide you with anecdotal evidence on the trials and tribulations of building a company. What these papers are missing are the intangible struggles that every successful entrepreneur has faced. Therefore, if your answer to the question of what you want is, "I don't know," or "I want to not work hard," then put this book down, and go get a desk job. Go work a 9-to-5 job, and do what 99.9999 percent of other people in this country do.

If you are not willing to stand up and fight for your vision, then don't waste your time reading *Small Business, Big Vision*. Luck is an accumulation of superior effort, and this book is no exception. Matthew and Adam have put their hearts and souls into it, as they seek to provide you with exclusive insight into the must-have tips, tricks, and knowledge necessary for you to accomplish your dreams.

If you want to work hard and achieve as much as you possibly can in business and in life, then this book is for you. Anything worth accomplishing never comes easily. As you will read countless times throughout *Small Business, Big Vision*, there isn't just one practical way to achieve your dreams. Instead, you must read this book through the lens of the question: "What can I implement that provides me with the driven, inspired, and relentless passion I need to crush it going forward?"

After reading this far, the question isn't whether you want to do this. The question is: Are you ready to stop at nothing to achieve everything? Only you can answer that question.

If you are ready, then *Small Business, Big Vision* will be your best friend alongside you in your journey. In addition, Adam, Matthew, and I are always here to support you, and so are all of the entrepreneurs who are profiled in this book. We care about you. Why? Because we know how tough being an entrepreneur is, especially in the face of mounting debt, and family and friends who don't understand why in the world you'd take on what is seemingly an unthinkable risk tolerance. Each of us has been there, many times over. So don't make the same mistakes we did. Learn from us, ask us questions, and be ready for the ride of your life.

Do you know what the hardest part about being an entrepreneur is? Keeping your flame going—in other words, transcending boundaries, creating an ecosystem of acceleration that catapults your business, leveraging knowledge, resources, tools, and contacts, as well as maximizing impact. That is a lot, and it is overwhelming. But the good news is that *Small Business, Big Vision* helps guide you through each of those daunting challenges.

Businesses come and go. But the journey you have begun is one that exudes a passion, persistence, and willingness to defy the odds that virtually no one in this world does. That makes you unique, special, and a valuable asset to us a reader, but more importantly, as a maverick in the business community. Take *Small Business, Big Vision* wherever you go, and absorb it. Have the confidence that you can do what you want in life. There is no rewind button. You only get one shot. So make it a good one—read this book, implement, execute, and send us an e-mail.

We look forward to sharing the journey with you.

Best regards,

Gary Whitehill
Founder, New York Entrepreneur Week (NYEW)
and the Relentless Foundation

Preface

When John Wiley & Sons, Inc., approached us to write a book based on our entrepreneurial experience, we thought long and hard about it. Many people would have jumped at the chance without a second thought, and we were no doubt flattered by the invitation. We hesitated, though, because when we undertake a new business project—whatever it is—we approach it with the objective to make a significant impact. The idea of publishing "just another book" on entrepreneurship to add to the thousands already in print didn't really appeal to us—and it was certainly not what our publisher had in mind, either.

We have been immersed in entrepreneurship since our early teens. We've bought companies, sold companies, boot-strapped, and transformed businesses that some people thought could never be saved. Today, we have one of the leading entre-preneurial Web sites in YoungEntrepreneur.com. Combined with our other Web and print properties, we have established a following made up of tens of thousands of entrepreneurs from around the world. We have an interesting story, and we know that our experience has given us a wealth of knowledge to share. However, writing an autobiographical story just isn't our style; we feel that it would be too self-centered. We therefore decided that we could only agree to write a book if we knew for sure that we had something important to share, and a unique way to present it, so that we could truly make a difference in our readers' businesses.

With that rather tall order in mind, we sat down and talked at length about how we would craft our book and what we could offer to readers looking for entrepreneurial advice. What you have in your hands right now is the result of not only the conversations and meetings we had about this book, but also nearly 40 combined years of uninterrupted experience as entrepreneurs.

What we realized in researching various options for this work was that people who are looking to start and grow a business want, more than anything else, two things: (1) nuts and bolts, practical advice on what to do; and (2) useful information about how to overcome the obstacles and challenges that everyone is sure to face along the way.

In the following chapters, you will find answers to the most frequently asked questions in the entrepreneurial world, such as: "Do I really need a business plan, and how do I write one?" "Should I hire people to help me run my business?" "Do I need to have investors?" "How do I make social media work for my business?" and much more. But not only will you find in-depth, useful answers to these questions, you'll also read profiles of entrepreneurs who asked the same questions themselves when they were starting out—and you'll learn how they found the answers as well.

These profiles will show you how various individuals put the information they uncovered into practice successfully in real-world scenarios. You'll read about Gabriel Shaoolian, founder and CEO of Blue Fountain Media—a man who has never taken a dime from investors, yet has been able to build his Web-design firm into one of the preeminent companies of its kind, catering to the likes of high-profile clients such as Procter

& Gamble, Nike, the NFL, and the United Nations. You'll learn how Matt Mickiewicz, founder of SitePoint.com, took 99designs from a thread on an online forum to a multimillion-dollar company—by not following conventional big business wisdom. And you will hear from many other well-known and not-as-well-known entrepreneurs who have made it happen and are willing to share the inside scoop on exactly how they did it.

Our intent is that the examples presented in each profile will offer evidence to substantiate the information we're detailing. After all, if it's not something you can use in your own business, it's really of no use beyond entertainment value. At the end of the book, you'll also find a list of resources to further support each chapter's topic and give you places to get more information and tools to further your entrepreneurial pursuit.

So, we set out to write a book of real value for all current and would-be entrepreneurs—whether you're about to start your first or fifth business, or you're looking for ideas to take an existing business to the next level. And we know this book accomplishes that goal in a big way. The bottom line is this: Read this book to find out what to do and how to do it, to see that it's been done before and how they did it, and to get the inspiration to go do it yourself.

Small Business, Big Vision is this book's title, the long-standing tag line of our Web site, YoungEntrepreneur.com, and the philosophy that has always driven us to push harder and accomplish more—often more than anyone else believed was possible. This philosophy says that although your business might be considered *small* for statistical purposes, you are only constrained by the size of your vision—not by your bank account, not by your SBA classification, and certainly not by the opinions or beliefs of those around you.

Thanks for getting our book. Let us know how it helped you in your entrepreneurial journey. We'd love to hear from you!

Cheers!

Matthew and Adam Toren

Acknowledgments

We want to acknowledge the help and support of our wives, children, mother, and grandmother. They have all been there to provide the positive encouragement and the motivation we needed to be where we are today.

We also want to thank the many entrepreneurs who have shared their experiences with us over the years. They have educated and inspired us and have given us the opportunity to pass on their knowledge to those who are interested in learning about entrepreneurship.

Last, we want to acknowledge each other. We come from a close family and have been fortunate to have this great brother-best-friend-business-partner relationship throughout our entrepreneurial journey.

Permissions

The authors wish to acknowledge and thank the following entrepreneurs for their contributions to this book:

Brock Blake of FundingUniverse

Adam Braun of Pencils of Promise

Ali Brown of Ali International

Anita Campbell of Small Business Trends and BizSugar.com

Scott Harrison of charity: water

David Hauser of Grasshopper Group

Shama Hyder Kabani of The Marketing Zen Group

Daven Michaels of 123Employee.com

Mike Michalowicz of *The Toilet Paper Entrepreneur*

Matt Mickiewicz of SitePoint and 99designs

Brent Oxley of HostGator.com

Mike Roberts of SpyFu.com

Dan Schawbel of Millennial Branding, LLC

Gabriel Shaoolian of Blue Fountain Media

Siamak Taghaddos of Grasshopper Group

Gary Vaynerchuk of Wine Library TV

Introduction

Why You Need This Book and Why You Need a *Big* Vision

It's no secret that there are a million business books out there. Almost anything you could ever wonder or want to learn about business is contained in a book somewhere—and you can track down anything that's not in one of those many books online.

Doesn't sound like we're making a great case for reading this book, does it?

Yet the truth is that although we've read a great number of books and are constantly reading blogs and other online sources, there still seems to be something missing to us. Sure, there are plenty of interviews with successful entrepreneurs all over the place; there are more than enough opinions about what you should and shouldn't do when starting and running a business; and there is even some helpful how-to style information here and there—for a price.

What's missing, as far as we can tell, is an approach that provides you with the information you need, explains how to implement that information, and also gives you some concrete examples of people who have applied the techniques presented—successfully. And that's why you need this book.

We are not just presenting theories and feel-good stories about millionaire entrepreneurs. Instead, we're providing you with real value—information you can implement in your own company, whether you're in pre-start-up mode or already thriving and growing. We're also giving you real-life examples of other entrepreneurs who have used the same methods to start and grow amazing businesses. These examples will show you that it's not only possible to use the information we've presented, but exactly how others have done so.

Throughout the book, we also focus on the importance of vision in building your business. Why is vision so critical? Regardless of the quality of the information you receive from other sources—and regardless of how inspiring you find the examples you read—if you don't maintain your vision for what you want your company to become, it's not likely to happen. Each entrepreneur we profile will substantiate that his or her unwavering belief is the single factor that has made all the difference in their success. Some of the people we've profiled have college degrees, and some don't. Some came from entrepreneurial backgrounds, and others didn't. A few of our entrepreneurs had a decent amount of start-up capital, while many scrimped, scraped, and bootstrapped their way to success. But one thing is common to each of them, and to every entrepreneur on the planet: Every single person who launches and develops a business faces obstacles and challenges along the way—period. There are no exceptions. You, too, will come up against opposition in many forms, often even from within your own head. And all the tricks, tools, and action steps in the world—no matter how sound they may be—won't help you one bit if you don't have the right outlook and a strong, clear vision.

Your vision is what solidifies your resolve when things get tough, and it's what clarifies exactly why you want to be in business in the first place. And having a big vision from the beginning is what makes it possible for you to know when you've finally made it. After all, your vision is all about knowing where you're headed; without it, how will you know when you get there?

Of course, many people will tell you that there is really no such thing as *getting there*. And there's some truth to the fact that the most successful entrepreneurs in the world often never really feel as though they're "done." True entrepreneurs don't relish the destination as much as the thrill of the journey. However, that doesn't change the need for vision—because vision is fluid. Having a clear picture of where you want to go isn't about laying down a rigid path from which you never waiver. It's about knowing what you want, and knowing that you'll do whatever it takes to get it. The "what you want" part might change, grow, or even morph into something completely different over time, but as long as it always represents what you truly want, you'll know that you are on the right track. There is a significant difference between people who change their goals based on new information or desires and people who are all over the place because they just don't know what they want. And that difference is vision.

Our Story

As we stated in the book's preface—we have no interest in writing an autobiography at this point in our lives. A book that's all about us would be contrary to what we're trying to achieve, so that's not what we've put together here. However, we do recognize that you might not have ever heard of us, and probably want to know a little about who's delivering the advice in the pages of this book. So here is our story "in a nutshell."

We grew up learning the entrepreneurial lifestyle from our grandfather, Joe. He actually set us up on our first entrepreneurial venture, selling little stunt airplanes at a local folk festival. He taught us the proper way to use the stunt plane to really wow the audience, and we sold out of them before the folk festival was over. What a great feeling for a couple of seven- and eight-year-old kids! So it began; the entrepreneurial bug had taken its bite.

We went from one mini-venture to the next throughout our school years. From importing stereo equipment to magic kits from Hong Kong, we learned a lot and made some money along the way. As soon as we graduated from high school, we took the money we had earned and bought a struggling billiard hall in an up-and-coming part of our town. This is where we learned the saying that you hear so often from entrepreneurs: "We poured our blood, sweat, and tears into that business."

We put in many long hours, undertook a huge rebranding, and devised a number of creative promotions for the venue. We eventually expanded it into a place where people can enjoy a game of pool and a nice glass of wine while listening to a live jazz band on stage. Our hard work, dedication, and creative marketing ideas allowed us to soon became the "place to be" on Thursday, Friday, and Saturday evening, and we had lines at the door nearly every night.

The buzz about this cool new nightspot continued building. We then started throwing private parties for the movie industry, as we had the ideal location and a big enough space to accommodate large groups. The steady stream of nightly customers, coupled with the corporate business we were able to attract, equaled success beyond anything we had imagined. Before we ended our first year in business, we had received an offer to sell. It didn't take long for us to realize that the long nights of sleeping on our venue's couches had paid off.

We took the deal and moved on to our next adventure, this time in a totally different industry about which we knew nothing: printing and graphics. We found a struggling downtown printing and graphics company, and we used the same philosophies and ethics to overhaul and brand that organization. Success came quickly again, as we sold it on our eleventh month in business for a sizable profit.

We took our graphic team from the printing company with us and then launched a publishing and media company, which has been one of our main focuses for the past five years. We have owned and operated several niche-market luxury lifestyle magazines in Canada, Arizona, and California. With a combined readership of more than 500,000 per issue, our venture in the publishing business has remained strong even while others in this sector have struggled.

We realize that some things haven't changed much since our first business venture. Our passion to help others launch, manage, and grow successful business ventures started early, continued throughout our early entrepreneurial lives, and drives us to this day. While we were working hard on some of our first business ventures early on, we were written up in several media outlets. The Junior Achievement Association took notice of this, and asked if we would be willing to speak to the local high school's eleventh and twelfth grade marketing and entrepreneurship classes about our experiences. As a result, we gladly began speaking to students on a regular basis. We were thrilled to share our stories, and regularly dedicated a few days every month to visiting community high schools and talking about the real-world entrepreneurship experiences we've had. It provides these students with a nice break from their textbooks, because it's always powerful to hear real stories from people who are actually living these lessons.

This rewarding experience compelled us to want to help as many entrepreneurs as possible. In 1999, we set out to build what has now become the largest and fastest-growing social networking forum for entrepreneurs in the world, YoungEntrepreneur.com. YoungEntrepreneur has since become a must-visit resource for startup CEOs, founders, aspiring entrepreneurs, mentors, and investors worldwide. It reaches an audience that few other Web sites can match. This model caused us to realize the great need for quality entrepreneurial resources; as a result, we began SelfMade.net earlier this year.

Our social network and blog properties also include Blogtrepreneur.com, which is dedicated to helping online entrepreneurs find success. The site showcases information on entrepreneurship, marketing, online business strategies, as well as interviews with entrepreneurs and a wide range of features, solutions, and support. We also help small business owners from a wide variety of industries start, run, grow, and even sell their businesses, through our consulting firm, Biz Warriors. One of our specialties is improving profitability of underperforming businesses with a unique bottom-line approach. Our consulting work also allows us to provide instruction in management concepts and finance to emerging and distressed small businesses, covering all phases of operations. In short, almost all of our efforts now are designed to assist small business owners with starting, managing, and growing successful business ventures.

One thing we've learned through all our entrepreneurial adventures is that good advice is priceless—and that's precisely why we wanted to write this book. It is our mission to help entrepreneurs succeed, and in the pages that follow, we will do our best to fulfill that mission. We've had many mentors and teachers along the way, and we hope we can do for you what they have done for us—provide the insight and knowledge necessary to make your entrepreneurial dreams a reality.

1

The Importance of Having BIG Vision

Good business leaders create a vision, articulate the vision, passionately own the vision, and relentlessly drive it to completion.

—Jack Welch

Entrepreneurs come from every conceivable background: every ethnic group, economic class, education level, and physical ability; almost every age group, and both genders. Some come from generations of business owners, while others are the first in their families to ever consider starting their own business. Among the ranks of those who call themselves entrepreneurs are inventors, programmers, and artists, while others excel at building teams, selling, or devising marketing plans. It is difficult to come up with a description of what a "common" entrepreneur looks like or acts like, or to pinpoint the necessary skills or experience one must have. In fact, there is an endless list of differences among entrepreneurs, but there is one thing all entrepreneurs have in common: *Vision*.

Why is vision a universal entrepreneurial trait? It is because the purest definition of an entrepreneur is: "Someone who starts a business with a great deal of initiative and potential risk." These individuals' willingness (and desire) to take that initiative and assume that risk sets them apart from everyone else in the world.

Every entrepreneur has experienced this feeling. Sometimes it's a spark that springs to life while brainstorming with a business associate; other times it's a surge of inspiration while in the shower, or that ah-ha moment that wakes you from a sound sleep. It's the first glimpse into the very essence of possibility— and the feeling is indescribable. Some people have even called it spiritual. The feeling takes hold the moment you sense that you're onto something amazing, and ignites when you realize it could be something huge. That realization—that picture in your mind of future possibilities—is what vision is all about. It's something on which you can expand to take your business from a mere inkling of an idea to a full-fledged, fully operational, thriving company. That's the feeling that overtook Dan Schawbel when he first imagined what his company, Millennial Branding, could become.

Entrepreneurial Profile: Dan Schawbel of Millennial Branding, LLC

To say that Dan understands what it's like to have a big vision is quite an understatement. At 27 years old, Dan is the youngest columnist at *BusinessWeek* and has been called a "personal branding guru" by the *New York Times*. He is the managing partner of Millennial Branding and the author of the number one international best-selling career book, *Me 2.0: 4 Steps to Building Your Future* (Kaplan 2009).

Dan is a founding member of the Young Entrepreneur Council, and writes syndicated media columns that are seen by more than 1.2 million readers biweekly. He has written articles for a variety of other print and online publications including the *Wall Street Journal*, *Entrepreneur*, *BrandWeek*, Mashable, AOL Jobs, Yahoo! Shine, MediaPost, BNET, and *Advertising Age*.

As a national speaker, Dan has spoken to high-profile corporations such as IBM, CitiGroup, Time Warner, Harvard Business School, and MIT, and is exclusively represented by the Big Speak Inc. speaker's bureau. Dan helps individuals and companies with creative branding solutions.

How Dan's big vision has evolved—in his own words: "When I first started out, I referred to myself as the 'personal branding spokesperson for Gen-Y.' I was careful not to use the word *expert*, because I was only writing about the subject on PersonalBrandingBlog.com at that point. After six months of hard work—and after establishing a magazine, online TV show, awards, and published articles—the magazine *Fast Company* profiled me. This led to Google

(*continued*)

(*continued*)

asking me to speak at their campus and my current company, hiring me to be the first social media specialist. It proved my theories about personal branding, and thus I rebranded myself as the 'personal branding expert for Gen-Y.'

"I eventually wrote my book, which is entitled *Me 2.0* and targeted at Gen-Y, but read by other generations. I officially launched my company in January 2010, and my vision has changed quite a bit since then. My firm is a full-service personal branding agency whose mission is to inform and educate professionals on the importance of personal branding so they can achieve career success and happiness in their own lives. The association my name has with personal branding has helped me tremendously in becoming top-of-mind in this field."

How Dan's unwavering vision has fueled his success:
"I can honestly say that I've never doubted myself when it comes to personal branding. I firmly believe that I was born to be doing what I'm doing now, which gives me confidence and alleviates any fear. I've been rejected and ignored so many times at this point that it doesn't even bother me! When you're confident about your product, you don't worry about failure."

The importance of having a Big Vision from the start:
"A Big Vision gives you a point on which to focus to create short-term, measurable goals. I always tell clients that you need to start with the end goal in mind if you want to take steps today to reach it. Brand yourself for the career you

want, not the job you currently have. If you can't envision the end product before you start creating it, you don't know what you will end up with. You will waste a lot of resources, time, and money if you don't know the exact product you want to develop. My greatest talent is being able to take a vision, turn it into a realistic model, and then execute on it. A big vision also gets both me and my team excited about the journey we're taking toward success and accomplishment."

Dan's advice for entrepreneurs interested in starting a company from the ground up: "Entrepreneurs who are starting a company from scratch should base their business on something they truly love. It's the only way you're going to work hard enough to reach your big vision. It's easy to give up and quit on a business that you're just doing for the money. Try to use the least amount of capital possible when you first start, because it will allow you to survive the first year. And finally, it's vital to surround yourself with people who can complement your skill set, and who you can trust."

How Dan defines success: "Success means putting yourself in a position that allows you to monetize your passion. You will be happy if you're making money doing what you love—regardless of how much money that is. True success comes when you wake up each day with the freedom and flexibility to do what you want, when you want, and how you want to do it. I feel like I'm in control of my own destiny, and that I positively change other people's lives as well."

Fuel Your Fire with Passion and Perseverance

Though an initial spark is an essential ingredient, there is much more to being a successful entrepreneur than having and maintaining that vision. The unfortunate reality is that there are plenty of people who have the "big vision moment" but who never become entrepreneurs—because they don't have the passion needed to sustain this vision long enough to take action. There are also people who get started but who lack perseverance, and therefore falter when obstacles arise.

Turning your initial vision into a viable business has everything to do with your level of passion and ability to keep moving forward, even in the face of challenges. Without passion, it is easy to become discouraged from pursuing your plans by other priorities and self-doubt when difficulties arise. Your mind-set ultimately dictates your actions, so operating with one that is anything less than dedicated unwaveringly to your future as a business owner will cause you to struggle to take the actions necessary for your success.

Every entrepreneur in the world comes up against challenges in his or her business. No matter how carefully you plan; no matter how great you are at what you do; and no matter how hard you try to make sure everything always goes smoothly, unexpected trials *will* test your vision. The many successful entrepreneurs we've interviewed from a variety of industry sectors, backgrounds, and areas of the world have almost all credited their *perseverance* as the most significant element of their success. They claim that their ability to maintain their vision and a positive mind-set in the face of adversity has been the X factor that has made all the difference in their eventual achievement or failure. Their vision was big enough to carry them through the hard times, so it overshadowed any doubt that crept in along the way. In fact, these kinds of challenges are exactly what cause many entrepreneurs to thrive.

But even the most formidable entrepreneurial spirits aren't immune to discouragement and disappointment. We all struggle at times to maintain our positive mind-set and to stay true to our initial vision. Fortunately, we can use unexpected setbacks and problems as opportunities and learning experiences, and we can push through just about anything. But let's be realistic: there isn't a person on the planet who doesn't, at some time, have doubts or worries about themselves or their business. It would be unnatural to *never* feel discouraged or frustrated. The key is to keep those feelings from ruining your vision and changing your mind-set. During the worst times, we can all use some help to persevere and stay the course. To that end, we present five keys for maintaining your vision and positive mind-set:

1. **Plan your work and work your plan.** Entrepreneurs commonly become discouraged by a sense of being overwhelmed. This is particularly true within start-up companies, or those experiencing a period of sudden growth. Although the start-up process can be an exciting, energizing time—and although growth is almost always a great thing—the pressure to get so much done in a short amount of time can mount and incite feelings of frustration and worry. In companies where deadlines are the norm, these feelings might not ever ease up. In fact, regardless of company structure, we can all occasionally feel like there just isn't enough time in a day to get everything done that needs to be done. So how do you keep from losing sight of your vision when this happens?

    One way to avoid, or at least reduce, the pressures that can dampen your entrepreneurial spirit is to stick to a plan as closely as possible. This isn't your business plan; rather, it's about a daily action plan that keeps you focused—not only on the details of your day, but on the big picture as well. A great way to devise such a plan is to ask yourself what you *have* to do daily to achieve your long-term objectives. Once you've answered that question, design your daily plan around those activities, and delegate or hire others to perform as many of the other tasks as possible.

There are some significant advantages to this tactic. First, chances are good that the duties you end up tackling will be those that have to do with building and growing your business. If you're in a business that you love (which is hopefully the case), you'll enjoy the activities that contribute most to the company's success. And it doesn't really feel like work when you're doing what you love to do, even if you have a ton on your plate—and you're far less likely to become overwhelmed. Additionally, working from a plan of action gets a lot of your "to-do" items out of your head and down on paper (or on a computer screen). You know what your responsibilities are and can focus on one thing at a time without all the other issues weighing on your mind.

Of course, even when you have a plan, you'll need to deal with some unexpected "fires" that come up. When these challenges arise, the key is to handle them as quickly and efficiently as possible, with the goal of getting back on the plan as soon as you can. Your plan can be flexible, but only to the extent that it continually supports your long-term vision.

2. **Guard against negativity—from outside *and* within.** No matter how intense your initial spark was, it simply isn't possible to maintain it for long if you're deluged with negativity and cynicism. This can be a difficult challenge to overcome at times, because it is often those closest to us—friends, family, and coworkers—who are the ones feeding us negative energy. This may especially be the case if you don't come from a family or peer group of entrepreneurs; you're more likely to

receive a lot of push-back from those around you and you might even feel some resentment as you experience success.

You can take steps to effectively offset any negativity you're experiencing, either from other people or from yourself. First and foremost, it's important to think for yourself and stay focused on your business and your dreams. You should certainly be open to others' feedback and criticism, but only take actual advice from those who have done what you want to do. People with whom you discuss your business idea frequently act like experts—even though they have never successfully created their own company. Just remember that the person with whom you're talking probably isn't qualified to advise you unless he or she has accomplished what you want to accomplish. Their hearts might be in the right place, but always take what they say with a grain of salt.

Surround yourself with positive people as often and for as long as possible. Attend networking events; get to know other entrepreneurs in your community; schedule lunch with a high-energy peer to have an inspired discussion about the future. Prioritize your time so that for every hour you spend around people who are negative, you spend two hours around people who "get it" and who can feed you positive energy.

3. **Fortify your mind.** Our culture's "self-improvement movement" has been in full swing for more than 35 years now—and enough material has come out of it to keep you surrounded by positive words for the rest of your life. An Amazon search for the term *self-improvement* yields more than 60,000 books, not to mention thousands of DVDs and audio programs in MP3 format and on CD. If this isn't enough, you can find countless seminars, retreats, workshops, and camps, all designed to infuse your mind with positive energy and purpose. On top of that, you have the option to

hire a business or personal coach to keep you focused on your vision.

Instead of watching the news (or almost any TV for that matter), listen to an audio book or watch a YouTube video of inspirational speakers like Les Brown or Tony Robbins. You have an opportunity to control what goes into your mind; choose to focus on positive, uplifting, and motivating material to help you overcome obstacles more easily, to ignore the negativity of the world around you, and to keep your vision alive and strong.

4. **Embrace change.** It's been said that the only thing you can count on never changing is the fact that everything changes. You can plan for every contingency imaginable and the unexpected is still bound to arise at some point. It is simply the nature of business and life. Whether it's an economic downturn, an unexpected product shortage, or new technology that changes the face of your industry, something will happen sooner or later for which you didn't—and couldn't—plan.

Often, the difference between thriving and feeling overwhelmed in such times of change is the ability to embrace the change and make it work for you. Rather than feeling crushed when things don't go as planned, stop and think of how this new or different set of circumstances can work in your favor. You'll be surprised at what you can come up with when you approach change this way. As you'll learn in this book, some of the best companies have come about as a result of their owners' need to completely reinvent themselves when faced with unexpected circumstances. What starts out as a challenge that has the potential to cloud your vision can ignite a new spark that you never would have recognized under other circumstances. So accept that change is inevitable, embrace it, and make it work in your favor.

5. **Let history be your guide.** Every successful person—from the Wright brothers and Walt Disney, to Thomas Edison, Bill Gates, and Donald Trump—has experienced setbacks, disappointments, and internal doubt. Although all of these individuals accomplished amazing things, each of them had to overcome obstacles, just like you do. What kept them going more than anything else was a belief in their vision, an ability to focus on their goals, and most importantly, a sense of perseverance that pulled them through when they needed it most. The encouraging thing is that none of these qualities is reserved for a select few; we can *all* access them.

If you're still having trouble staying motivated, do whatever you need to do—whether it's reading an inspirational book, staring in the mirror and giving yourself a pep talk, or sitting on a rock meditating—to recapture that original feeling you had when the spark first hit and your vision was crystal clear. Remembering that moment—and, most importantly, reestablishing that frame of mind—will get you through any challenge you face. No matter what the world throws at you, you do have the power to push through. So don't let anything or anyone get between you and your *BIG Vision*!

Take a cue from entrepreneurs Siamak Taghaddos and David Hauser, who faced more than their share of challenges in building Grasshopper Group.

Entrepreneurial Profile: Siamak Taghaddos and David Hauser of Grasshopper Group

Siamak Taghaddos and David Hauser are great examples of entrepreneurs who saw a need and had the big vision necessary to fill that need—and then some. Back in 2003 there was no solution available for the kind of phone system they were looking for, so they decided to build it themselves. Today, Grasshopper—"The Entrepreneur's Phone System"—is one of a suite of products offered by David and Siamak's company, Grasshopper Group. To date, they have served more than 100,000 small business owners looking for a robust, economical, professional way to stay in touch wherever they go. With the buzz that Grasshopper has generated throughout the entrepreneurial community and business media, it's clear that these professionals know a thing or two about making their vision a reality.

However, the strongest evidence of their amazing ability to accomplish a vision might just be their success in getting President Obama to declare a National Entrepreneurs Day. They created the proposal, launched a campaign, promoted it, and got it done in less than six months. As a result, President Obama announced the celebration of the United States' first National Entrepreneurs Day on November 19, 2010. Now *that* is big vision!

How Siamak and David have pushed forward when faced with challenges: Siamak: "Even at our lowest points, neither David nor I had any doubts. We always engaged in very relaxed conversations that went something like this: 'We're about to face XYZ disaster if we don't do something about it. Here's what I'm thinking. . . .' And we'd simply make some changes or take care of the issue. Our un-wavering confidence in our own ability to simply fix prob-lems surprises me sometimes. Panicking is the worst thing a leader can do."

David: "When bootstrapping a company, you defi-nitely run into challenges and bumps. But that is also what creates a great company, and as an entrepreneur, you must believe in yourself and your team's ability to overcome those hurdles. It is a lot like a roller coaster; many times you could jump off at the bottom and crash and burn, but entrepreneurs are the ones who say, 'No, I am going to make a change or continue pushing forward and make it happen.'"

The importance of having a Big Vision: David: "It is very important for an entrepreneur to have an idea of what 'success' looks like to them and to always be pushing toward those goals. But the most important element is their ability to communicate that vision to others so they can buy in and all work toward that shared vision. Unless everyone in the company is moving toward the same goal, the objec-tive will never be realized. It is just as important for busi-ness owners to understand the changes along the way, and appreciate the fact that the final result might be close to but not be *exactly* what they originally had in mind."

Siamak: "A clear vision is the most important thing for an entrepreneur to have. Successful people always have an idea of where they want to be, and do everything they can to reach that place. It's the same reason why I think people go to fortune tellers—they need someone to give them that

(*continued*)

(continued)

same vision that comes naturally to entrepreneurs. The important thing to keep in mind, however, is to never get lost in that vision. You have to be flexible enough to change and evolve it if needed as you move forward."

Siamak's and David's advice for entrepreneurs interested in starting a company from the ground up: Siamak: "Be resourceful and always remember the acronym JGSD: Just Get Sh** Done. Want to create an app? You can get it done in a few weeks. Want the President to declare a National Entrepreneurs Day? We did it in less than six months. Want to get on the cover of the *New York Times*? Start making some phone calls. Whatever you want to do, just figure it out and get it done."

David agrees: "Stop talking, go out there and *do something*. Anyone can talk about great ideas, but entrepreneurs bring them to life and get someone to pay them for it."

How Siamak and David define success: David: "Success for me is empowering entrepreneurs to succeed, empowering team members to do amazing things, and creating a profitable company that will be around for a long time."

Siamak: "Achieving your goals, and being content in your personal and professional life."

2

Rethinking Your Business Plan

Business plans are a great section in the science fiction genre. They are made for the kind of people who like sausages and don't know how they are made.

—Yossi Vardi, investor and entrepreneur

Ah, the business plan. One of the most discussed—and most misunderstood—facets of starting a company. It also can stop a would-be entrepreneur in his or her tracks. Just the thought of creating a 50- to 100-page document with facts, figures, and graphs supported by polished, important-sounding text—along with all of the other "necessary" elements of a formal business plan—can overwhelm anyone. It is tragic to think of all the great business ideas that are surely out there in people's minds that will never see the light of day because their creators think they need to write a long, complicated business plan before they can do anything else.

Would-be entrepreneurs who feel that they need a formal business plan do have options. They can research information on how to create one, and try to do it themselves. However, many people are much better at devising and implementing ideas than they are at generating documents. The mere thought of having to write a formal business plan can be completely uninspiring for anyone who is excited about building a business, but not necessarily thrilled about *writing* about it.

Another option is to pay someone else to write your business plan. This is actually a great alternative, as long as you choose wisely when deciding who will create it—and as long as you have the funds to do so. However, entrepreneurs who are bootstrapping and watching every dime might find that spending a few thousand dollars on something other than marketing, equipment, or product development is slightly off-putting, to say the least.

Still, many people will tell you that it doesn't matter if you don't know how, don't want to, or don't have the funds. Like it or not, they will claim, a formal business plan is the first thing you must create before taking another step in the start-up process. These folks believe that anyone who starts a company without first devoting some serious thought and time to writing a comprehensive plan—which must include all the essential "traditional" plan elements—is doomed to fail. To these people, starting a business without a formal plan is equivalent to taking a cross-country trip without a map (or GPS). They believe that without a complete plan, you'll be all over the place, with no direction or idea of where you're headed or how you'll get there. You'll run into obstacles you never saw coming and have no idea how to deal with them. And, they say, don't even *think* about trying to get any financing!

The underlying point that these purists are trying to make in cautioning you to first build a business plan and then build your business is one we hear often (and one we happen to believe is very true): "Those who fail to plan, plan to fail." So are they right? It makes a certain amount of sense, doesn't it? After all, it is true that having a clear picture of where your business is headed can only help you get there, not hinder you. So without a good business plan as a "roadmap," maybe you *are* indeed destined to fail. You might even think that the difference between the 50 percent or so of companies that make it past their first year in business and the other half that don't lies with whether they started with a formal plan. But if you think that, you will be surprised by the actual statistics.

A study undertaken in 2007 by Babson College sheds some interesting—perhaps even shocking—light on the subject. Entitled *Pre-Startup Formal Business Plans and Post-Startup Performance*, the study looked at 116 businesses started over an 18-year period, from 1985 to 2003. The study found that business survival rates and other measurements of success showed *no difference* between the performance of new businesses launched with or without written plans. Surprising as these statistics are, they indicate that unless a would-be entrepreneur needs to raise start-up capital from banks, venture capitalists (VC), or angels, there is no compelling reason to write a detailed business plan before launching an enterprise.

What does this mean? Is planning unimportant? Should entrepreneurs simply run out and start companies without performing any market research, creating a plan of attack, or giving the entire process any forethought? That would be like entering a boxing match with a blindfold on, and we don't think that this study—or our past experience—recommends that *anyone* do that. In fact, we believe that planning is absolutely necessary to starting and running a successful business. Even those people who believe that you can proceed without a formal plan will advise you to think things through, research the market, investigate the competition, and, yes, plan your business. What the study *does* suggest is that it's time to rethink the notion of a traditional business plan.

The One-Page Business Plan

What we have found to be true—and what countless serial entrepreneurs already know—is that although the planning process is critical for success, it does not have to result in planning paralysis. This is what happens when entrepreneurs get so hung up on designing their business that they can't move past the planning stage. It's a common problem, one that's partly perpetuated by the false belief that a formal business plan is a must-have for every business. The Babson College study shows that entrepreneurs can be successful without a formal, written plan; however, it doesn't prove that entrepreneurs don't need to plan *at all*. What they do need is something that falls somewhere between a tome-like document that no one will ever look at in its entirety after it's finally finished, and a complete lack of planning.

A goal without a plan is just a wish, and we absolutely advocate putting together a well-thought-out written plan. However, most businesses don't require this to be a two-inch-thick document; in fact, it can usually be as short as a single page. That's where the one-page business plan comes in. The one-page business plan is definitely a plan, but one that lets you actually begin running your business. The focus moves from planning *to plan to do* business to planning to actually *do* business.

Although it's called *a one-page business plan*, some of the plans that fall into this category can end up being two or three pages; however, they don't usually need to be more than that, and most are a single page. These one-page plans have specific elements that are designed to guide entrepreneurs through the start-up process, and to help keep things going once their business is up and running. These plans don't contain the extraneous material that you often find in a traditional business plan—and although you'll want to create financial projections, conduct market and feasibility analyses, and do some other number crunching, you won't include that stuff in your one-page plan. All of that information is important to know, but your plan is meant to end up as a document that will help to guide you—something to which you can refer along the way that will keep you on track. All those numbers, facts, and figures are good for telling you whether you've got a good idea and if it makes sense to proceed in the first place, but they aren't essential elements of a highly focused plan. Like any good plan, your one-page business plan should be a fluid document that will change as your business does. It is actually meant to be used, not simply created for the sake of creating it.

Before we get into the specifics about how to create a one-page business plan, we need to clarify something: We are big on bootstrapping, so much so that we've even devoted the entire next chapter to the concept of starting your business without the use of outside financing. However, we know that there are times when going after investor money or other forms of financing are necessary, or just make sense. These are situations in which a formal business plan is necessary. Yet even then you will find that creating a one-page plan is a great idea for internal use and can be a good starting point from which to build a more formal plan if and when you need it. Additionally, if you walk in and plop a 100-page document on an investor's desk, he might just tell you to take a hike if you expect him to read the whole thing. Much like the executive summary of a traditional business plan, the one-page plan is a good introductory document for providing an overview of your business. You can then bring out the beefed-up version for the loan committee. With that said, the following section provides details on how to put together a complete, functional, one-page business plan.

The Five Elements of a One-Page Plan

A one-page business plan contains five essential elements that come together to form a clear picture of what your company is all about, where you want to go, and how you plan to get there. Again, this is a fluid document, one that is meant for you to use and to review on a regular basis. That means that although the core elements of the plan will stay the same, you will probably tweak and update the contents as your business grows and changes.

Vision   As we emphasized in Chapter 1, you must begin with the end in mind. The vision section of your plan should start things off by describing what you're building in a high-level sense. Whether your goal is to dominate your market or simply be the best at what you do, this one- to three-sentence statement describes your primary objective. Think of it as the crystal ball that tells your company's future.

We stress throughout this book that vision is vitally important to every entrepreneur. If you were to write your plan to look like a pyramid, the vision section would sit at the top, supported by the other elements. Everything else you do is directed by what your vision statement describes. In fact, this becomes a useful tool in making business decisions, because each element should ultimately depend on the answer to one question: Does it support your vision?

Mission   Your vision describes your efforts' end result, but your mission statement details the reason for your company's existence. It discusses in broad terms what you will do to accomplish your vision. Mission statements often describe levels of service or quality of product, which makes perfect sense. If your vision is to dominate your market, for example, your mission will be to provide the kind of products and services that will lead to that market domination. Remember, you're creating a one-page plan, so keep it descriptive enough to tell the story, but brief enough to make the point quickly.

Objectives   This section supports your mission and vision by detailing the objectives that will lead to your achievement of what you wrote in those statements. You can do this simply by listing bullet points that state your business goals, such as, "Hold a 15 percent market share by the end of this year," or "Hire a full-time sales person by the beginning of the second quarter." Make your goals as specific as possible, and attach time frames to them. However, you shouldn't worry about providing too much detailed information in this section; just list end results. You aren't concerned with how you'll meet your objectives until the next section of your plan.

Strategies   Your strategies describe *how* you plan to achieve the objectives you set in the previous section. Again, you're keeping this to one page, so it isn't necessary to go into great detail. Simply list bullet points that explain your plan for reaching your objectives. One might be, "Build a strategic alliance with the Chamber of Commerce and other local business organizations to increase local visibility," or "Maximize gross profit by utilizing co-op advertising with select vendors" could be another. Notice that each example contains a statement—"Increase local visibility," and "Maximize gross profit"—which can refer to specific objectives you set for your business in the previous section. The key is to tie each section of your plan to the piece before it in a way that allows you to drill down from your ultimate goal, all the way to the action items needed to get there, which brings us to the final section of your one-page business plan.

Action Plans   It's a good idea to use bullet points in this section as well. Again, although there's no need to be overly descriptive, these items will have specific dates tied to them and offer more details than the bullet points in your strategies section. An example of an action plan might be: "Negotiate bulk rate pricing with XYZ Manufacturing and have new pricing in place by March 15." An action plan like that could support a strategy of, "Offer cut-rate pricing to all new customers," which might support an objective of, "Increase market share by 5 percent by June," which could support a mission of, "Offer customers the lowest price available," which might be in support of a vision that says, "To be the number-one provider of (fill in your product or service here)." You can clearly see how each piece of the plan supports those above it.

So there you have it—the one-page business plan. Unlike the kind of document you put together for investors and financial institutions, the one-page business plan is light, practical, and easy to review. It won't take you three months to put it together; it won't cost you a fortune; and the thought of creating it isn't enough to keep you from starting a business. You might even consider keeping it posted on the wall above your desk to remind you where you're headed and how you plan to get there.

Still feeling a bit overwhelmed? Anyone who's looking for proof that you can build a real business with a one-page or less business plan will find it in the profile of HostGator.com's Brent Oxley.

Entrepreneurial Profile:
Brent Oxley of HostGator.com

If you've been on the Internet for any time at all, chances are you've at least heard of HostGator.com; you might even use them to host your own Web site. As host to more than 200,000 sites, and with annual revenue in excess of $80 million, a company of this magnitude—you might think—must have started with a first-rate business plan. But HostGator founder Brent Oxley tells a different story.

Brent launched HostGator out of his college dorm room, and like so many Internet success stories, he didn't even imagine that his company would become one of the industry leaders within a few years. So the thought of creating a big, formal business plan wasn't even on his mind. It's interesting to hear Brent's claim that—even knowing what he knows now—he would not go back and start with a traditional business plan if given another chance.

Why Brent didn't start with a formal business plan: "A business plan would have been way too professional! I didn't even have a name picked out when I decided to start a Web-hosting company. I dealt with the reality of my situation; I was young, poor, and in college. There are only so many businesses you can create with a $1,000 budget, and Web hosting happens to be one of them. I had very little experience with hosting and even less when it came to running a business. I winged everything, used trial and error to figure out what worked—and turned HostGator into the $80 million a year business that it is today."

(*continued*)

(continued)

The balance between underplanning and falling into "planning paralysis": "There obviously has to be some type of plan or strategy. [It] can be just a few thoughts, an idea, or even based on pure luck if that's the angle you're taking. The less people you have involved, the more freedom you're going to have. If you have partners, it's more important to have a defined business plan, because you need to make clear what everyone's role will be and what their goals are, [and include] some type of timeline as well.

"The most important words of caution for any business plan: Expect the unexpected. In other words, you can't plan for everything, [so] you have to be ready to adapt and take action [when something you haven't anticipated occurs] I [encounter] businesses every day that have everything planned out to a tee on paper, and [most of them] have the same problem. They spend more time planning and meeting than making concrete decisions and acting on them. By the time they implement their plan, someone has already done what they want to do, or the business environment has changed to a point that their plan is completely outdated. When it comes down to it, there is such a thing as too much planning.

"If I could go back and do it over, I wouldn't change a thing. I didn't know what I was doing or where the business would end up taking me. But if I had spent most of my time planning, I would have missed out on the most important part of getting started, which was gaining experience from trial and error."

Brent's advice for entrepreneurs interested in starting a company from the ground up: "I've learned a lot building HostGator, and have the following advice for anyone who starts a business:

- Always be honest and fair with your customers. A company's reputation is everything, and will mean the difference between success and failure in many cases.
- Live as prudently as possible. The more you reinvest in your company, the more you will reap in the future.
- Have as few partners as possible—even none! The more partners you have, the higher chance you have of failure.
- Trust and count on no one [besides yourself]. If a job is going to get done, you're more than likely going to have to do it yourself.
- Don't sell too soon. I constantly see entrepreneurs sell the second they begin to become successful. They get a quick buck when, with just a little more time, they could make millions.
- Be personally available 24/7, 365. If you aren't available to help a customer, the competition will be."

How having a Big Vision has played a part in Brent's success: "Having a Big Vision [causes] me to constantly demand more from HostGator. Without vision, I'd quickly become content with the success we've experienced and give up striving to hit new goals. Vision has also allowed me to stay focused on what *I* believe the future will entail rather than what the competition says it will be."

The Finance-Centered Plan

Now that we've taken a good look at the kind of business plan that applies to most entrepreneurs—the one-page business plan—let's talk about the business plan you'll need to create if you intend to get your company financed. As we stated earlier, even if you intend to raise money from an angel investor, venture capitalist (VC), or bank, it's still a great idea to create a one-page business plan to use as a foundation for your full-blown plan.

Even though traditional business plans often contain a lot of information and are more comprehensive than the one-page plan, we still believe they can be simple and straightforward. We've seen plans that are up to 200 pages, and the fact is that this length is almost never necessary. Just because you have a lot of information about your market, competition, or financial projections, this doesn't mean that it all has to appear in your business plan. Your goal isn't to overwhelm your audience with facts, figures, and information; it is to convince them of two things: (1) that your business is viable; and (2) that you have the ability to make your objectives a reality. Potential investors need to know that your idea is sound and will produce a good return on their investment, and that you and your team have what it takes to pull it off. That's it.

So how do you create a plan that assures them of both these things? It's easier than you might think. The following are the eight necessary elements of a finance-centered business plan:

1. **Executive summary.** Your one-page business plan primarily forms the core of your full-fledged plan's executive summary, which many say is the most important part of any business plan—and we agree. Even though all portions of your plan can hold a great deal of importance in the long run, the

executive summary is the section that typically determines whether an investor will even bother reading the rest of your plan or not. The executive summary sells your plan, and, as the term suggests, *summarizes* exactly what your proposed business is all about.

Because this first part of your business plan is so vital, you must be sure to take time to create a killer one-page business plan, and then craft it into a winning executive summary—which should only be about two pages long but packed with a lot of power. Many people think it's best to create your executive summary last to be sure it accurately summarizes and reflects the rest of your business plan. Even if you don't take this approach, do make sure that you revisit it after completing the rest of your plan. Again, it's important to realize that bankers and other potential funders are only going to look at the first few pages before deciding whether to consider your business further. Make certain that you've given them enough information in the executive summary to decide that both you and your business idea are good investments.

2. **Business overview.** This section of your plan outlines your business idea, what you plan to offer, and which methods you plan to use to sell your products or services. This is a high-level overview of your business concept that paints the picture of what the business will look like. It should also include where the business will be based, if you'll have a brick-and-mortar location, a Web site, and so on, as well as the legal form (sole proprietor, LLC, S Corp, etc.) you'll use for the business.

Unless you have a complicated or unusual business model, you can usually keep this section to a page or two. Don't make the mistake of going off on tangents here and start detailing how you'll market your business or why your products and services are needed. There will be plenty of opportunity to do all that in the following sections.

3. **Management.** Remember when we said that you're not only using your business plan to sell your business idea but yourself, too? This is where you have a chance to explain how you and the other individuals involved with your company have what it takes to make it a success. The people behind the idea are at least as important to any potential investors as the idea itself, so make sure that you have a strong team, and sell it in this section. List each key member of your management team and highlight his or her accomplishments and experience as they pertain to steering your company toward profitability. You'll basically be listing each team member's résumé; however, keep the focus on facts and concrete information rather than the oft-seen résumé fluff. You'll find that many top companies do a great job at describing their management teams on their Web sites, so it's well worth some time to scour the About Us sections of businesses you admire to get ideas.

   Another piece of advice: don't try to cover up any missing pieces or personnel. If you know your team is lacking in a particular area like human resources, for example, address this rather than trying to skirt the issue. All of the options available these days for virtual assistants, remote workers, and outsourcing companies should allow you to fill in most small gaps. On the other hand, if you're missing a key player—like someone who can build and implement an effective marketing plan—you'd better get busy headhunting!

4. **The market.** No matter how much you might be in love with it, your idea is not that great if there isn't a market for it. Someone who is contemplating investing in your business

needs to know that the marketplace has a genuine need for what you plan to offer. This is a question you need to answer for yourself as much as for any investor. Before you can offer any product or service, you need to assess the need for it—and figure out as well who exactly will be buying what you're selling.

Doing extensive research on your industry and the key target demographics will not only ensure that a market exists, it will also help you discern where to go when it's time to promote your offering. Part of this section will also detail your potential competition. Again, this is a topic you want to find out about, even if you aren't trying to get investor money. Once you've established that a need for your products or services exists, and determined both who your buyers will be and with whom you'll be competing, it's time to create a detailed plan on how to market to your target audience.

5. **Sales and marketing strategy.** By this point, you've outlined your business concept, showcased your stellar management team, and made a convincing case that there is a genuine need for your company to exist. Now it's time to explain exactly how you plan to reach the market you discussed in the previous section. After all, you can have great products, outstanding service, and a first-rate management team, but none of that matters if no one knows you exist. This section will end up serving as the outline for your company's marketing plan. It will explain how you'll spread the word about your products and services—whether that's through a sales force, traditional media like television and radio, online advertising, social media, or a combination of these tools. Though there is a place for social media in just about every company's marketing arsenal these days, it isn't

the only approach, so be sure you aren't excluding other strategies that could help you drive business.

You will also want to create a unique sales proposition (USP), which is a statement that defines what about your company will convince someone to choose you over the competition—and it can't always be based on the lowest price. It's rare that being the "low price leader" makes sense for a USP, and investors typically don't like to see this as a strategy. You should approach your business in a way that shows you're in it for the long haul—because you are! So make sure that your marketing plan reflects strategies that support relationships and loyalty.

6. **Financials.** This is often the most difficult part of putting together a business plan for many entrepreneurs. Although preparing financial statements and projections can be daunting, this section is essential if you're interested in getting financed; after all, it's what banks or investors are most interested in. If you are not yet conducting business, you should include your assets and liabilities, and your projections for income, expenses, and profit. If you have already started, this section should include current financials as well as future projections. Though these projections are always somewhat of a guess by their very nature, they obviously need to be based on real data, and you'll need to clearly explain and to be prepared to justify on what information you've based your numbers.

The good news is that even if you don't have a clue how to start this process, there are plenty of resources out there to help you, many of which are free. We've included some links at the end of the book that make it easy to access the Internet's vast information base, to help make this process a breeze. Whatever method you use to create this section, be sure that you and your key management team are familiar with the information contained in the section. You don't want to be caught off guard if you find yourself in a meeting with an investor who asks a question about the numbers. You want investors to get the impression that this topic is just as important to you and your team as it is to them. Although it's true that money isn't everything, that's not the sentiment you want to convey while sitting in front of investors.

7. **SWOT analysis.** You might be familiar with SWOT analysis if you took a business course in college. SWOT stands for Strengths, Weaknesses, Opportunities, and Threats. In the context of a business plan, it is simply a way to show potential investors that you've thought through your idea and accounted for every possible contingency. Even if this is your first time ever hearing of this process, don't worry—it really is simple to compose a SWOT analysis. The best way we have found to get through this step is to start with four blank pieces of paper, each with one of the four SWOT elements at the top. Start making a list of everything that pertains to your business that falls within each category. Next, review the list and expand on each idea you wrote down until you've covered it sufficiently. Then polish it up, put it all together, and add it to your business plan. It really doesn't have to be more complicated than that.

Many people tend to downplay the "Weaknesses" and "Threats" portions on the SWOT analysis. It's akin to being asked for your biggest weakness in a job interview and answering, "Well, I guess I'd have to say that I'm obsessively on-time and I just work too hard sometimes." Remember, you're creating this plan as much for yourself as for the investors, and you really do want to take an honest look at any areas where you can improve or where your execution might not be up to par. As long as your weaknesses and threats don't blow up your whole concept—and as long as you have a plan to address them—anyone looking at your SWOT analysis will admire that you've thought of everything. What you *don't* want is for someone to bring your attention to a disadvantage that you hadn't considered. So be thorough.

8. **Additional supporting documentation.** At this point, your business plan is almost complete. This last part is for any additional documentation that supports your plan, clarifies its contents, or strengthens your position. For example, include copies of any certifications you have that are necessary to conduct business here. If you have a signed buy-sell agreement on a piece of property on which to construct a widget-making facility, put that in this section. If you have previous business experience for which you've received awards, accreditations, or press coverage, be sure to include all that in this section as well. This final section of your business plan is your chance to show your potential investor that you really have thought of everything, and you're completely prepared and capable of making them some money!

There is no question that the process of building such a comprehensive business plan is time-consuming and can be overwhelming for many entrepreneurs. This can cause what is sometimes referred to as *planning paralysis*—which is the primary reason we strongly advocate that most start-ups design the one-page business plan. But, there are times when it is necessary to create a traditional plan. If and when that time comes for you, it makes sense to expend the necessary effort to do it right. Take the necessary time to pour all you've got into the process. After all, getting financed makes all the difference in the world as to whether some businesses become the next big thing, stay a mom and pop, or even make it at all. Of course, whether to go after financing is an important question in itself, which is why it's the subject of our next chapter, and the specialty of our next entrepreneurial profile, Brock Blake of FundingUniverse.

Entrepreneurial Profile: Brock Blake of FundingUniverse

Brock Blake is the CEO of FundingUniverse, a company established in 2005 to help make the angel investing and small business financing industries more efficient by increasing the amount of completed deals across the nation. Brock knows what investors are looking for and has helped countless entrepreneurs in their quests for funding.

Brock has received several awards of recognition, including the #2 Startup to Watch Award from *Business Q* magazine, and Utah Technology Council's 2007 Emerging Executive of the Year. *Utah Business* magazine recognized Blake at age 24 as one of the "Top 40 Under 40" business professionals in the state. Additionally, his peers selected him to vSpring Capital's prestigious v100 list in the years 2006, 2008, and 2009. Brock currently serves on several advisory boards, including the Utah nonprofit organization LaunchUp, the Utah Valley Entrepreneurial Forum, *Launch* magazine, Brigham Young University's Collegiate Entrepreneurs Organization, and Weber State University's Entrepreneurial Society.

Brock discusses what investors are really looking for in a business plan: "The truth about business plans: Entrepreneurs hate to write them and . . . investors hate to read them! During my time at investment services FundingUniverse and Lendio, we have helped thousands of entrepreneurs connect to banks, credit unions, angel investors, venture capitalists, and other funding sources. The interesting thing about playing matchmaker is that you quickly discover various perceptions and inaccuracies from both sides of the table.

"One of the most essential things to remember: Keep your business plan *concise*. The key to a well-written business plan is that your target audience (investor, lender, etc.) should be able to quickly find and consume the most important information. Most of the time, this means that the document should be less than three pages; in fact, some of the best plans that I have seen were only one page. Focus your attention on the topics that portray the best attributes of your company and do your best to keep the plan concise and easy to comprehend.

"Also, remember that most investors are trying to find the next Google or Facebook. In order for a company to grow that quickly, the addressable market size needs to be large and growing. Make sure that you do your research and are able to communicate the details of your market opportunity in your plan."

Brock's advice on what to expect if an investor is interested: "After an investor has expressed interest in further discussions, you'll want to have the following items prepared for the next phase of due diligence:

1. **Historical financials.** If you have already generated revenue, investors will want to see your historical financial statements (including income statement and balance sheet) to get comfortable with the company's past performance and future forecasts.
2. **Detailed financial plan.** Most investors will look at your three- to five-year financial forecast to get a glimpse of

(*continued*)

(continued)

how you think as an entrepreneur. They like to look at the growth assumptions and expense forecasts, since doing so helps them gauge the likelihood of future success.

3. **Meeting the team.** While many angel investors and venture capitalists spend most of their time interacting with the CEO, they will also want to spend as much time as possible getting to know the rest of the executive team. At the end of the day, their decision to invest usually relies heavily in the amount of confidence that they have in the entire team's ability to execute on the plan.

4. **Market and customer research.** Once you complete steps one to three above, investors will usually ask to talk to current customer references. This helps them validate the market demand and customer need.

5. **Legal review.** Once the investor has successfully completed all other due diligence items—and if he or she is still on track to invest—they will usually bring in an attorney to review the legal aspects of the business. Those items will likely include a review of the incorporation documents, customer contracts, employment agreements, option agreements and any related 409A issues, outstanding lawsuits, et cetera."

Brock's take on how investors have changed with the economy: "Raising money has gone through some interesting highs and lows over the past few years. When the economy crashed in October 2008, early-stage investing came to a screeching halt. Because most investors had lost a significant amount of money in the stock market and/or real estate market, they became gun-shy and conservative on the higher-risk investments. As a result, it was almost impossible to raise money at the time.

"Since capital wasn't flowing, entrepreneurs had to focus less on their business plan and more on their actual company. While difficult at the time, most believe that the market's tightening has forced business owners to focus on solving real-world problems that will generate revenue quickly. As a result, many great companies started to emerge and investments started to flow again. The main difference now was that most businesses that were still in the idea stage (without any real traction) were deservedly being overlooked by the companies that had bootstrapped their way to generate revenue and customers."

Brock's advice for entrepreneurs interested in starting a company from the ground up: "Do it. There is never a better time than now to build a business. And focus on three things:

1. Solving a true customer pain.
2. Sales. Revenue cures a lot of sins.
3. Talent. Surround yourself with people who are smarter than you."

How having a Big Vision has played a part in Brock's success: "At the end of the day, having a Big Vision is what drives your success. Building a successful business is full of the highest of highs and the lowest of lows. If you aren't passionate (or determined and stubborn) about your

(*continued*)

(*continued*)

vision, then it's unlikely that you'll stick with it long enough to become successful."

How Brock defines success: "Success to me is first defined by relationships. For me to be successful, I must have a strong relationship with my wife and children. No amount of [professional achievement] could make up for failure in the home. Success [means] building long-lasting relationships with family, friends, partners, co-workers, and customers. If that happens, financial success will follow."

3

Investors Out— Collaborators In!

In the long history of humankind . . . those who have learned to collaborate and improvise most effectively have prevailed.

—Charles Darwin

The last chapter ended with an explanation of how to create a business plan to present to investors. Therefore, it might seem strange that we are now saying—"Investors out." However, this chapter's focus isn't to tell you to *never* bring on investors. Rather, it emphasizes the importance of knowing when it makes sense and when it doesn't, what you need to know when and if the time comes, and the importance of finding genuine collaborators—not just deep pockets.

Despite our personal preference to avoid investors, we're not always opposed to the idea of bringing them on board or going for other forms of financing. There are times in the evolution of some companies when it makes sense to secure outside money. However, this definitely isn't true for every company; we would even argue that it isn't the case for the majority of entrepreneurial ventures. Many of the most successful entrepreneurs we know have bootstrapped their way to success without ever utilizing external financing. This has been the case for most of our own companies as well.

The mistake we often see entrepreneurs make—and the issue we address in this chapter—is the idea that you *must* find outside money in order to start a business. If you read business magazines and blogs and follow other sources of start-up news, you'll find plenty of stories about companies that have secured first- or second-round financing. You'll also read a lot about how to find investors, which sectors are hot for investors right now, and how to structure your company or write a business plan to attract investors. It's easy to see why an entrepreneur might think it's necessary to secure financing in order to start a company. However, this just isn't the case.

Investors: A Question of Need versus Want

We believe that the answer to the question, "Does it make sense for my company to look for investors?" is a matter of need. In other words, it's important to take an honest look at your company's objectives and your options for reaching them to determine if you must acquire financing in order to do so.

The key word here is *need* not *want*. You might picture your company operating out of a high-end office building with 150 employees, each with a top-notch health-care plan and the latest computer on his or her desk. There is nothing wrong with envisioning that goal. However, if it's possible for you to operate out of your one-bedroom apartment or your garage for the next year until you have some revenue rolling in, then you probably don't *need* any of those things right now. We all want to have our vision realized sooner rather than later, but it can be a big mistake in many cases to bring in investors rather than patiently building your business at a slow, steady pace.

Common Reasons for Entrepreneurs to Seek Investors

There are many reasons why entrepreneurs feel a need to look for investors. Let's look at some of the most common, as well as some questions you can ask to determine if you are dealing with a need or a want.

Enhanced Office Space   We see this one all the time. Many people think that having a proper office somehow legitimizes their business, so one of the first things they do is run out and sign a lease. But the truth is that unless you're opening a dental practice or another business for which you must have a professional office, you can start almost any business without one. Some of the most successful companies around—Amazon and

HostGator, for example—began in their founders' garages or dorm rooms.

Even if you must meet with clients, remember that plenty of business is conducted at coffee shops every day, and it isn't uncommon to meet at someone's home office. If you're thinking that you need an office because you plan on hiring employees— well, just keep reading.

Ask yourself the following questions to help determine whether you *need* office space:

- How can my business be run from home?
- What alternatives are there to office space?
- If an office is necessary, would a co-working space be just as good?

Employees   Another expense that many entrepreneurs take on before it's necessary is payroll. As with office space, this often goes back to the feeling that having employees makes your business a "real" company. We've devoted an entire section of this book to dispelling this misleading notion. For now, let's say that employees are not necessary for most businesses for a long time, and many never have to hire anyone, ever. With all the options available for outsourcing, virtual assistants, crowdsourcing, and so on, there's much that you can accomplish without paying for full-time help.

Questions to ask:

- Can a virtual assistant or other outsourced solution do what I need?
- Is there any real advantage to hiring employees at this time?
- Are the perceived advantages to employees outweighed by the expense and headaches that come with putting people on the payroll?

Equipment   Depending on your industry, you might need specific equipment to run your business. And no matter what your area of business, at a minimum, you'll need a computer. But some entrepreneurs find that they have champagne tastes and a beer budget when it comes to buying these supplies. For example, let's say that you're starting a printing company and want to purchase a $150,000 Heidelberg printing press. If you don't have the money, you don't have a business, right? Well—that might not be the case. The first thing you need to do in this situation is examine the alternatives. First, you can probably purchase a used press for a fraction of the cost of a new one. And although you might want a Heidelberg, compromising with another lower-priced manufacturer might work until you can afford to upgrade. For that matter, maybe you don't really need a press at all. You might consider getting started by outsourcing or reselling, and build up a large enough client base to be able to afford to open your own shop.

Questions to ask:

- What is the minimum with which I can get by for now?
- Can I secure a short-term lease or buy secondhand?
- By thinking outside the norm, is there a way to build this business without equipment?

Remember, this book is largely about vision. It's vital to maintain that great vision of what you want your business to be, so we're not telling you to give it up. We *are* saying that it makes sense to consider the various paths that can lead to that vision. And if one of those paths includes building your business without outside money, that's a course you should follow for as long as possible.

There are some significant reasons that we feel it's best to avoid this option for as long as you can—and in many cases, forever. Again, we don't have anything against people who invest in companies. In fact, some of our good friends are VCs and angel investors. Most investors have their hearts in the right place and have a genuine desire to build successful companies. But even when you find an investor who is a good match, you have to be ready to give up some things that many entrepreneurs aren't ready to relinquish. Depending on the deal you strike, you can expect to make concessions that range from handing over a piece of your company when it comes time to sell, to completely giving up control over everything you do and how you do it. Entrepreneurs are notoriously independent, and letting someone else tell you how to build and run your baby can be difficult, to say the least. Additionally, as we discuss shortly, not every investor is looking out for the best interests of you and your company. In the meantime, if you want a clear example of what someone can accomplish without taking loans or investment money, just have a look at what Gabriel Shaoolian has been able to do.

Entrepreneurial Profile:
Gabriel Shaoolian of Blue Fountain Media

Gabriel Shaoolian has an amazing entrepreneurial success story. He is a consummate entrepreneur who built his business from scratch, with no outside funding or unusual advantages, and has made it to the top of his market. As founder and CEO of Blue Fountain Media, Gabriel is doing what every entrepreneur dreams of doing: He's making his vision a reality.

After working for some prominent Web-design firms in New York City, Gabriel decided to go out on his own, first as a freelancer, and then by starting his own firm. Rather than acquiring investors or other sources of funding, he started Blue Fountain small, reinvested in the company, and grew—slowly at first, and then more rapidly as word about the firm's high-quality work got out. Today, Blue Fountain Media's client list is a testament to its vision, drive, and patience. Serving big names like the NFL, Procter & Gamble, Nike, and Disney, the company has, to this day, never taken investment money or outside funding.

Why Gabriel is glad he didn't take on investors: "You have to have *some* capital to begin with. You can't expect to make a salary, because in most cases, you won't be doing so for a long time. So you've got to have some funds to fall back on. The first thing you notice when you go into business is that you have this wonderful thing called *overhead*—and you have a lot more of it when you grow than when you are a freelancer. You have to be prepared for everything from insurance to corporate taxes, to making sure that everything is in place with benefits, networking, etc. All of these things will creep up on you, and you have to have money to handle them.

"But even with that said, I'm glad we didn't bring investors on board; it really put the responsibility on us as a team to bring in next month's revenue. There is a tendency when you have an investor for people to get too relaxed, since you're operating under the knowledge that somebody else owns you. Because we didn't take on investors, we control our own destiny. We feel more accountable for our work, and we are more proud when we succeed. I don't think you should bring an investor on board until you have a process and a system in place and you want to grow rapidly. But when you are starting out, they are more of a hindrance."

Gabriel shares the importance of advisors: "The best advisors I've found are the ones that motivate me to get my business to the next step—people who succeeded in their business. An example is British advertising executive, David Ogilvy. I read his book on advertising that he wrote about 40 years ago, and the rules he includes still apply today. He talks about looking for 'good' clients, because a 'bad' client will drill you into the ground. A good client understands what you offer and appreciates the value you provide. Taking on a bad client—one who doesn't pay and constantly demands free work—can become very problematic, very soon.

"The other people who I consider my best advisors are the ones who emphasized how much courage it takes to be an entrepreneur. They told me it takes balls to run a business. You've got to take risks, because if you don't, you are not going to grow. It's also important to remember when

(continued)

(*continued*)

taking advice that the people offering it should understand your business."

Gabriel's advice for entrepreneurs interested in starting a company from the ground up: "First you have to know how to define your business. What is your value? What makes you stand out? You should be able to explain this in a single sentence. For instance, ours is, 'Results-driven Web design, development and marketing.' The 'results-driven' is what makes us distinct. We produce sites that achieve specific business results; our marketing gets our clients' companies on the first page of Google results. You have to know what makes you stand out in a crowd.

"I once went out with a client who said, 'I like you, you do good work. But why *you*?'

"You know, I struggled with that answer for two years. When I tried to answer him, I went all over the place. First, I said, 'I care.' But all business owners care. That's why they went into their own business in the first place.

"Then I said, 'I try harder.' But, again, most business owners try very hard. Then it dawned on me: What differentiates us is that we deliver projects that are results-driven. You have to know your business's audience and figure out what makes you stand out to that particular group. You must know your value proposition and how to explain it and then have the processes in place to deliver. Even when I hire people, my focus remains on finding individuals who are results-driven. I set out specific goals for everyone who works for me. Working very hard or very long hours is not good enough unless you are delivering results."

How having a Big Vision has played a part in Gabriel's success: "The motivating factor for me was that I wanted to become that *known brand*. I could have stopped when we had 20 people, or even 40 people. But I wanted to be the biggest name in the Web-design and marketing business. I wanted to walk into a party and have people immediately recognize our business's name when I told them, and know exactly what we do. This is what motivates me. I know that we're not even scratching the surface right now. That's part of the fun, but it's also a big part of the stress. You have to ask: Where do I see myself in five years? In five years, I want to be running a company of which everyone in the U.S. knows the name. No one has cornered that market in the Web world the way H&R Block has for tax preparation."

How Gabriel defines success: "Success comes to different people in different ways. On one level, success is laying out your goals and hitting them. That's the technical answer.

"There is also an emotional answer: Success is doing what motivates you . . . and what makes you happy. Believe me, I am married to my company and it gets really stressful at times. You don't have a life when you're an entrepreneur. When you go on vacation, you get to the hotel and immediately start thinking, 'Well, what's their system? What are their processes? What kind of software are they using?' You are constantly thinking about business. You are never on a break.

"But you know what? You have to enjoy it. If you don't, you won't feel successful. Part of the hero's path is going on that journey. It's the journey, the challenge that must not only drive you, but that you must enjoy."

When Your Needs Call for Investors

Though we recommend that you try to build your business without investors for as long as possible, there comes a time for many companies—even right at the outset, for some—when the company does have genuine needs that can only be satisfied by seeking outside funding. Some examples are:

- **Sales are strong—*too* strong.** Some companies find themselves in a position where they're not able to keep up with customer demand for their products due to lack of funds for production. Although this certainly doesn't seem like the worst problem in the world at first glance, your whole operation can fall apart if you don't quickly get the money to ramp up your production.

- **Your company has outgrown you.** Many entrepreneurs' main strength is their ability to produce amazing ideas. Some are even very good at implementing those ideas. However, many entrepreneurs have no clue how to actually run a company of any substantial size. At some point, it often makes sense to bring in outside help in the form of a CEO, COO, and/or CFO. It might be necessary to up the ante in order to attract the kind of talent you need for these positions, and to do that, you might need to get financed.

- **You need a prototype.** If you've invented a new gadget or application, you'll likely need to create a prototype to get it patented or otherwise legally protected, or to sell the idea to buyers. The costs associated with these processes can vary widely, and you typically need to do it all before you start generating revenue. If you don't have the personal funds to make all this happen, finding investors might be your only option.

- **You need equipment.** Let's return to the print shop example. You might explore all avenues and still find that you need specific equipment for which you just don't have the money. You can finance some supplies through the manufacturer, but even in these cases, you might need to find investors to help cover down payments and other associated expenses.

- **General start-up expenses.** As Gabriel Shaoolian explained, every business has overhead, and you need a way to cover it. If you don't have the money to start your business, you might need to find outside money. Of course, if you don't have any "skin in the game," so to speak, VCs will be reluctant to even speak with you. However, there are some angel investors—and other sources like friends and family—that you can consider in these situations, as long as you have a sound, well-thought-out concept.

All of the above examples describe a scenario with a genuine need to secure some kind of financing. When you've explored your options thoroughly and bootstrapped all you can, and you just aren't able to accomplish what you need to without outside money, then seeking investment money is your best course of action.

Collaboration Is Key

Once you've made the decision to search for outside investments, look for more than just "someone with money." If you find yourself in a position where you're desperate to get funded—and therefore jump at the first offer that comes along—you are likely to regret the decision down the road. Remember: Although there are plenty of honest, up-front VCs and angels, there are also investors who are not exactly altruistic and are only after a quick return at any cost. There are some shady characters out there, and too many entrepreneurs have gone from the elation of securing investment money to the agony of losing everything, in short order. The hard part can be telling the good from the bad—and making the mistake of working with the latter can destroy your business and your life.

Even "angel" investors don't always live up to their titles. Many of these people are unfortunately predators in disguise that are not looking out for an entrepreneur's best interests. Others aren't quite as malicious but lack the skills, connections, or experience to be of real value to you and your company. Some entrepreneurs make the mistake of believing that as long as an investor has money, it doesn't matter what other qualifications they bring to the table. But seeing an investor as nothing more than dollar signs is shortsighted and naive. It is rare to find someone who is willing to put up significant amounts of cash and remain a truly silent partner. And even if you do find that kind of investor, why wouldn't you want more? It's far more valuable to your company to find someone who can provide financing *and* help you reach your goals by offering expertise, support, and guidance.

The important part is to make sure that the goals investors are helping you reach really are *your* goals. You don't just need investors for that; you need collaborators. And in order to find collaborators, you should be as selective in choosing an investor as they are in deciding whether to invest in your company. Don't grab the first offer of financing, and don't feel like this investor should have total control. Set the tone for your future relationship from the beginning, and make it clear that you are not just looking for money, but also for someone who is a good fit for your company. In reality, selecting an investor means selecting a partner, and a partner needs to share your goals, philosophies, and vision for your company. It is someone who wants what you want. When either of you wins, the other wins, too.

Learn about your potential investor's background, successes, and failures. Get in touch with other entrepreneurs who have worked with him or her; they can tell you if getting involved with that investor was a dream or a nightmare. They can also give you insight into how the investor works, their level of involvement in decision making, and if they followed through on their promises and obligations. You need all of this information to help you make an informed decision and protect both your own and your company's interests.

Before making a final decision to bring on any particular investor, make sure you sit down and lay out exactly what you're looking for and what you expect the collaborator's role to be. Neither of you wants to be surprised six months down the road when you're too far in to turn back. It's also important to be willing to defer to the investors in the areas of their expertise. After all, their experience and knowledge should be part of why you want them to come onboard. So although you don't want to take a completely subordinate role, don't get so confident that you resist help and advice. True collaboration is a two-way street, and all parties need to be willing to work together toward your Big Vision!

An Advisory Board as a Replacement for Investors

There is one final option that is a fantastic alternative to bringing in outside investors: find people willing to collaborate with you and invest their time and expertise *instead* of their money, and build an advisory board. This option might not get you the equipment you need or the big office you're hoping to move into, but it is a great way to build a team of professionals to guide you. If you've been thinking of taking on investors so you can afford to hire an executive team, this alternative is worth some serious consideration.

When you go out in the business community and network with other company owners as part of your business-building efforts, you are bound to meet seasoned professionals who have the knowledge your company needs to get to the next level. Although you might not have the capital to persuade them to come on board as employees, you might just be able to convince them to join your advisory board.

To begin putting this group together, first make a list of the business areas where you can use the most assistance. Common categories might include marketing, sales, operations management, and finance. Get a clear idea about the specific help you need in each of these areas; discern what kinds of skills, knowledge, and connections an advisory board member would need to have to help fill these needs. Also, your advisory board members—just like your investors—need to be made up of people with whom you feel comfortable working and who share your general business philosophies.

Next, decide on what you will expect from an advisory board member, including the time commitment they will need to make on a monthly basis, and how long a "term" on the board will last. You should also determine whether it is acceptable for members to participate long distance, or if they should be physically present for every meeting.

Once you know what you want from your advisory board members, think about what you can offer them in return. Though this might vary from one person to the next, it should be consistent. The possible variations on this piece are nearly endless. Some people who serve on advisory boards don't get anything beyond the satisfaction of helping a fellow entrepreneur, while others do it in exchange for a piece of the company. You can come up with any number of possible scenarios between those two ends of the spectrum. For example, you could consider offering whatever products or services your company sells at reduced rates, or for free, to advisory board members. You want your members to take their roles seriously and give you their best, but you have to be sure that you're not giving away the farm. If you are truly using an advisory board in place of investors, think about what you would give up to an investor and keep that in mind when deciding what to offer to the board. Remember as well that you will need to create an agreement that stipulates exactly what board members are receiving and expected to contribute. You might want to consider making the first member of your advisory board a corporate attorney to help with this piece!

After you've determined what you want and have to offer from your advisory board members, it's time to go out and find them. As you did when looking for investors, you must be selective when filling advisory board spots—so talk to a lot of people and choose wisely. Again, networking is a great way to meet potential board members, but don't limit yourself to that avenue alone. Put a call out on your social media networks. LinkedIn is a good choice for this, as it is geared to a more professional crowd than some of the other platforms. Also be sure to ask other business owners for referrals, and check with your local SCORE (Service Corps of Retired Executives) chapter. Make the goal of your first contact with a potential candidate to simply set up a meeting to talk. You are building a relationship, so don't go right to the pitch. If you've followed the rest of the advice above, you'll know who you're looking for, so take the time to get to know prospective members. Figure out what questions you want to ask, and find the answers through conversation, not interrogation.

Whether you end up seeking financing now or at some point in the future, creating an advisory board of trusted, experienced professionals will help you take your business wherever you want to go. And if you do need financing at a later time, one of your advisory board members might just be the one to step up to the plate.

If anyone knows the value of advisory boards, it's business leader Anita Campbell, our next featured Entrepreneurial Profile.

Entrepreneurial Profile:
Anita Campbell of Small Business
Trends and BizSugar.com

As publisher of several online media properties and syndicated content sources, Anita Campbell reaches well in excess of 1,000,000 small business owners and entrepreneurs annually. She is the founder, CEO, and editor-in-chief of the award-winning online publication "Small Business Trends." The site has won the Forbes' Best of the Web twice (2005 and 2008), and has been highlighted on MSNBC's *Your Business* multiple times. Anita's media properties also include BizSugar.com, a popular social-media site specifically for businesspeople and entrepreneurs, as well as a weekly Internet radio/podcast show.

Anita currently serves or has previously served on a variety of boards, including the NorTech advisory board; Center for Information Technology and eBusiness (CITe) at the University of Akron; advisory board for NEOSA (Northeast Ohio Software Association); the Network Solutions Social Media advisory board; the British Airways Face to Face initiative advisory board; and various boards for private companies. She is also a prolific writer and speaker on the topic of small business, and is the co-author of the book *Visual Marketing* (John Wiley & Sons, Inc., 2011).

What makes an advisory board successful, according to Anita: "The most effective advisory boards are based on mutual respect. Specifically, they have the following two things in common:

(continued)

(*continued*)

1. **Show mutual respect.** Business owners must have respect for both their advisors' expertise and their advisors' time. Schedule regular meetings and run them efficiently. If you say a meeting will take two hours, don't go off on tangents and let it drag on for three or four hours. Prepare for meetings in advance by having an agenda and sticking to it. Send information for board members to review in advance, so they have a chance to think about it before the meeting. Include a recap from prior meetings to let board members know that you have acted on matters previously discussed; this demonstrates that you value their input. Keep phone calls brief and infrequent. In other words, acknowledge the importance of your advisory board members' time and input.

2. **Don't take undue advantage of board members' expertise.** Understand that an advisory board, especially one working with little or no compensation, is not there to take the place of employees or outside service providers. Don't expect members who are marketing consultants, or software programmers, or lawyers to develop your next marketing campaign, write code, or provide legal advice. They are there to *advise*, not *do*. If they offer to be hands-on in a small project, that's another matter altogether; and, of course, you would welcome their contribution. But don't expect it. Don't even put them in the uncomfortable position of having to say no."

Anita's most important criteria for advisory board members: "When choosing advisors, pick individuals who:

1. **Represent a wide skill-set and significant experience.** You want a range of expertise—because you're going to need it! You need a full arsenal when you're starting or growing a business: sales, product development, marketing, financial management, fundraising ability, people skills, technology, legal advice, and more. You'll bring some of these skills to the table, and your employees and outside service providers will provide some as well. But it helps to have a sounding board of those with expertise in as many areas as possible—and especially in areas where you and your internal team are the weakest. Sales and finance can make the biggest difference in a start-up; if nothing else, these two areas should be among your top priorities when looking for expertise.

2. **Aren't afraid of speaking their minds.** No 'yes men' or 'yes women'! Look, it's up to you to decide what to do with the input you get from your advisors; you can always choose not to follow their advice. Unlike a board of directors, an advisory board has no legal authority to overrule you. So you need not fear power struggles. But you do yourself a disservice if you never hear what you *should* be hearing. Pick advisors who will tell it to you straight, and give solid useful input. The stronger your personality, the more powerful your advisors need to be.

3. **Have big Rolodexes.** Go to your advisors not only for their ideas and advice, but also for the contacts they provide. It's a huge advantage to have advisors who can help you get a phone call returned from a prospective customer or business partner. This does not mean that you should pester them constantly for new introductions;

(continued)

(continued)

after all, you don't want to go to the well too often. Nor does it mean that you should expect to get customers solely as a result of the relationship that an advisor has. Contacts are for opening doors, not closing sales. But do recognize the advantage of a well-connected advisory board.

4. **Can devote sufficient time to the board.** I've been overcommitted to too many advisory boards at once, and had to retire from some. I simply didn't have enough time to do my role justice. Make sure to outline the time commitment to your advisors up front. Initiate a discussion if you notice that someone isn't available for more than one meeting in a row or isn't returning your phone calls. Let your advisors know that it won't affect your long-term relationship if they don't have the time to devote to an advisory board three or four times a year (or however often you expect to meet). Even make it clear that they can take a temporary hiatus until they have more time. It's better to do that than have advisors in name only; the apparent disinterest will feel demoralizing, not only to you as the business owner, but also to the other advisory board members. Absentee advisors are the kiss of death!

5. **Bring your company credibility.** Last but not least, choose advisors who are well known in your industry or who have a proven track record of launching companies, getting funding for start-ups, or growing organizations to the next level. This can bring credibility to your company. By getting involved with your business, your advisors are telling the world, 'This company is worthy of

my time and attention . . . and, therefore, should be worthy enough for *you* to buy from, go to work for, or partner with.' "

The Two Most Common Mistakes Entrepreneurs Make with Advisory Boards

Mistake #1: Playing politics with your advisory board. "Don't try to pit one member against another, or against your investors or partners. Sadly, I was once on an advisory board where the business owner invited me to lunch and then afterward to his office, where he proceeded to complain bitterly about another advisory board member. That member was also a minor investor in the company, and provided office space to the business owner. Yet here the entrepreneur was, sitting in free office space provided by that other board member/investor, complaining about him! Needless to say, I was extremely uncomfortable and resented being put in that position. The investor/board member was an acquaintance from the business community, and I felt that the owner's attempt to divide loyalties and create intrigue had put me in a difficult spot. As soon as I could, I excused myself and left. I then resigned from the board of advisors in a terse e-mail.

"But there's more to this sordid little tale. It turns out that a secretary had overheard the entrepreneur's complaints and promptly told the investor, who in turn evicted the entrepreneur from the premises for which he was paying.

"The lesson for entrepreneurs: You are bound to have disagreements with investors, business partners, and even other board members. Don't try to enlist your board

(continued)

(*continued*)

members as allies in these conflicts. They will lose respect for you if you try to pit them against another board member or investor or someone else key to the business—especially when those people are also the advisor's peers in the business community or industry. And, as it did in this situation, it could backfire on you—big time! Advisory boards are not a group with whom you should play business politics."

Mistake #2: Not using your advisory board's capabilities. "I've been guilty of this one: establishing an advisory board only to realize later that I did so too early or didn't have the time to really use my board to their fullest capabilities. You can't get value from advisors if you don't take enough time to convey information and seek their input. Recruiting an advisory board and then failing to use it is a colossal waste of effort."

Why Anita chooses to become a member of advisory boards: "Simply put, I learn a lot and develop new contacts by participating in advisory boards. Particularly as a small biz owner myself, it's too easy to get caught up in the day-to-day issues of your own company. You develop tunnel vision. Meeting with other board members and hearing about the challenges other businesses are facing helps you put it all in perspective. It's like taking a few deep breaths; you're rejuvenated in a small way. And sometimes you'll suddenly discover the answer to an issue you are facing in your own business by hearing others discuss a similar issue at a board meeting."

Anita's advice for entrepreneurs interested in starting a company from the ground up: "Divide the revenue in half, double the expenses, and triple the time to get it off the ground. This means that you should set some funds aside for living expenses and funding your business before you start it. If you don't, you'll probably run out of runway before the plane leaves the ground. Most companies fail because they run out of cash. They might have been successful given enough time. But their founders will never have a chance to find out."

How having a Big Vision has played a part in Anita's success: "A Big Vision helps drive you initially, and gets you to make that leap into starting a company. But no matter what your vision, chances are your business will change once you launch it. Entrepreneurs often don't understand what business they're really in until they've been in it a year or more. No matter what you thought it would be, it will probably morph into something different, depending on the opportunities that present themselves. Statistics bear this out; quite a few businesses have started out in one industry and ended up doing something different.

"Lesson: Be flexible enough to jump at promising opportunities, no matter what your original idea was. But be smart enough to detect the difference between a promising opportunity, and 'a hope and prayer.' You must evaluate these opportunities carefully, lest you end up chasing rainbows and never getting anywhere."

How Anita defines success: "Success as an entrepreneur is many things. For me, it's the following:

(continued)

(*continued*)

- Creating something you can point to that's lasting and bigger than you—a recognizable brand.

- Providing employment opportunities to others, including family members.

- Being profitable, and achieving the point where you no longer lose sleep about how you will make payroll this month or pay the company bills.

- Being profitable enough that you and your family can live a comfortable lifestyle."

4

Hiring Employees

The Good, the Bad, and the Alternatives

Don't hire. Until you are getting less than six hours' sleep per night.
—John Buckman, founder of Magnatune.com
and BookMooch.com

To those who have never managed a workforce, hiring employees can seem like the best option for accomplishing all that a busy entrepreneur has to do—and for getting it done in far less time than it would take alone. Ideally, this would always be true. In a best case scenario, having employees would allow you to get more done and reach your business goals more quickly and efficiently.

Employees can also help by performing the responsibilities that you would rather not carry out. For example, if you are most skilled in the areas of marketing and sales, chances are good that you are a creative thinker and probably aren't a big fan of tasks like accounting. Hiring an employee to take over the bookkeeping part of the business will not only free up your time to focus on those activities that are most important to building your business, it can also make your life more enjoyable by eliminating a duty that is not your main strength or preference. Most importantly, by allowing you to multiply your efforts through time leverage, hiring the right employees can be the next best thing to cloning yourself.

The Magic of Leveraging Your Time

Time Leverage—one of the greatest concepts in business—is the idea that you can exponentially increase the effort that any single person can put forth by adding multiple people who all perform the same tasks or who each take on specific, individual tasks. You pay for this type of increased productivity in the form of wages and benefits; and just like with everything else you do

79

in your business, you need to make sure the returns outweigh the costs.

Here's a simplified example of how this works: Let's say you make baskets and sell them to the general public. It takes you an average of one hour to make a basket, which you sell for $30; so essentially, you're making $30 an hour. Unless you are a basket-making machine, you are maxed out at around $100,000 a year in gross income. Not a bad wage—except that in order to earn it, you need to work almost every day of the year for 10 hours each day. If you're human, you probably aren't going to do much more than that.

On the other hand, what if you could hire five people who could produce baskets for you? You pay them each $15 an hour and continue to sell your baskets at $30 apiece. Each employee works for 40 hours a week making baskets, and you focus your own efforts on marketing and growing the business. Your gross revenue is now $312,000 a year, and after paying your employees, your income is $156,000 a year. Most importantly, you have freed up a great deal of your time.

Even though there are factors that this scenario doesn't consider—such as cost of goods and other overhead expenses—the numbers paint a clear picture of the power of time leverage, no matter how you slice it. The bottom line is that leveraging your time properly will result in more time for yourself and your family, more time to work on building your business, and ultimately more money in your pocket.

The Downside of Hiring Employees

Hiring employees is beginning to look like a fantastic idea. But hold on—there are other things to contemplate when you're considering amassing a staff. First of all, there is a great deal of expense involved in recruiting, hiring, and training employees. Yes, they can ultimately lead to greater time leverage and more income; however, due to various payroll taxes, benefits, workers' compensation insurance, training, and recruiting costs, it can take quite a while to realize the financial payoff. Another monetary consideration comes to light when you recognize that employees almost never match your level of commitment to your business, so they are often not as productive as you are. We can't really blame them for achieving lower levels of production than an owner would, but when that one-hour basket becomes an hour-and-45-minute basket, your profits will suffer. Employees also miss work occasionally and need vacations, all of which can affect your company's productivity.

In addition to financial considerations, one of the biggest challenges of having employees is *managing* them. Even seasoned supervisors can find this draining, and it can quickly become overwhelming for anyone without human resources experience. This isn't to say that all employees are slackers and ne'er-do-wells. In fact, it is possible to find conscientious, hardworking, loyal staff members who will be real assets to your company. It isn't always easy to find those people though, and it isn't as easy as you might think to differentiate the good from the bad. And when you end up with an employee who isn't doing your company any favors by being there, it isn't as easy as you might think to get rid of them. Depending on where your business operates, you might run the risk of wrongful dismissal lawsuits and all kinds of other legal trouble, even if you feel like you've done everything right. These issues can range from costly to devastating to your business, and there is only so much you can do to predict or avoid them. Some companies operate forever without any serious employment law issues, while others get hit with a lawsuit that drains the company coffers for good—even after making every effort to operate by the book. Though this might sound like an exaggeration, we've seen it happen, and it is definitely something you want to avoid.

Ali Brown, the entrepreneur featured in our next Entrepreneurial Profile, shows us what kind of a company is possible without hiring employees—if you do it right.

Entrepreneurial Profile: Ali Brown of Ali International

Ali Brown is CEO of Ali International, an Inc. 500–ranked company that provides advice, resources, and coaching to 50,000-plus women entrepreneurs around the world via programs, events, publications, and her Web site, AliBrown.com. Ali was one of Ernst & Young's Winning Women of 2010, one of 2010's Enterprising Women of the Year, and recently named one of Forbes' Women to Watch. You may have also seen Ali this past spring on ABC's *Secret Millionaire* show.

Ali's authoritative and unique business-building insights are big draws on the international stage; entrepreneurs all over the world seek her expertise. Ali hosts entrepreneurial events that change lives, and her workshops are unlike any other seminars. Everyone from stay-at-home moms, new business owners, to fully fledged savvy corporate divas, receive Ali's innovative success tools to help them take their businesses and lives to whole new levels. But perhaps most impressive is the fact that Ali has accomplished all this without an office. In fact, she did not hire her first employee until her company was well into seven figures in annual sales.

Ali's philosophy behind hiring (or not hiring) employees: "I never thought of myself as a business owner when I started to work for myself about 11 years ago. I was a freelance writer who was just trying to get by. So the thought of even hiring *any* help back then was extremely daunting! I soon hit a wall, though, and realized that

(continued)

(*continued*)

most of my time was getting sucked up by 'administrivia'—organizing receipts, paying bills, invoicing clients, going to the bank and the post office, making phone calls, or setting appointments. I was smart enough to figure out fast that even though I felt I could not afford to hire anyone, I would be in big trouble if I did not. Because if I kept going as I was, I would not have any time to *make* money!

"Once I knew I was going to hire, my next problem was figuring out how to fit someone into my 600-square foot, prewar NYC apartment—a place so small that the bed folded up into the wall and the bathtub was in the kitchen! There wasn't even room for *me*. Then a friend told me about Virtual Assistants—freelancers who take care of all that busy work for entrepreneurs like us. Because VAs are independent themselves, they work on an as-needed basis from their own homes or offices, saving you the cost and hassle of hiring a regular office assistant.

"This was the perfect solution for me during my first several years of business. I got to still work from home by myself while building a team of part-time contractors who worked from their own homes as well. My main revenue streams at this point were Internet-based; I sold e-books, courses, et cetera, online for women entrepreneurs. I then added on mentoring programs, and live events. I built my company to over a *million* dollars a year during this time, using only VAs—and it worked great for me."

Why Ali finally decided to bring on employees: "When I finally made the decision to bring on employees, it was because I wanted to move faster! I got to a point where a part-time team could not work quickly enough, and I wanted a dedicated staff. I didn't like hearing that any of my team members were working on projects for other clients or weren't available when I needed them. So I realized it was time to assemble a full-time team of dedicated employees. I was well aware this would come with many more headaches, including legal issues, taxes, extra paperwork, providing benefits, and other managerial hassles. But I knew our increase in speed would dramatically be worth any of these extra inconveniences.

"Finally having a dedicated team changed my business for the better. It took me out of the part-time mind-set into being a business leader, and made me step up and truly become CEO of my company. I was already leading tens of thousands of women entrepreneurs online via my mentoring and coaching programs, but now I was also leading my company. Today, I have eight full-time employees who are the rockets that support my ideas."

Why Ali doesn't have an office to this day: "My team and I friggin' love working from home. I love rolling out of bed, putting on some sweats and my Ugg boots and puttering around the house in the AM while checking my e-mail, or going for a rollerblade in the middle of the day, if it's a relaxed week. Most of my team members are moms, and they deeply appreciate the ability to be somewhat flexible with their hours and be closer to their families. They also save the money required for commutes and an extensive work wardrobe. There are so many advantages if you are game for this model.

"However, you need *strong* team members to pull this off. Because you can't look over someone's shoulder all day,

(continued)

(continued)

you have to trust they are working. You need staff members with a strong work ethic, who are self-motivated, good communicators. You need systems and checks and balances to ensure that they're getting the work done and moving forward on projects. Technology, of course, is the virtual team's Holy Grail. We have used extensive programs like Basecamp for project management as well as simple Google calendars, and it's a constant growth process learning what works best for us. We use the phone system OneBox to centralize our customer service, and people have no idea when they call in that we aren't all in an office together. And we use Box.net for our file sharing.

"It's also important to realize that you won't bond as much as a team when you are all remote. I have noticed that my younger team members—these gals in their twenties—do seem to crave that social aspect of work. So I realized it's important that we get together at least once a month when possible for meetings and/or some fun. We have employees in California and Massachusetts (simply because I live in California and my business partner Liz lives in Mass). So Liz keeps the East Coast team bonded as well. Once or twice a year we *all* get together, especially during my big annual fall conference for women entrepreneurs (called SHINE.)"

What Ali would do over with regard to the hiring: "We learned early on to *not* advertise that any of our positions are work-at-home. You attract all kinds of crazy people who are not qualified for the job. You don't want anyone interested in the position solely for that reason, and it could even turn some people off. So we learned to advertise for the position, and then during the interview process ask if the person was set up to work from home. Most of them are delighted to learn that they can avoid commuting.

"We learned to pay attention to those red flags you may notice in your initial interactions with potential employees. The situation never gets better when you ignore them; the damage is already done, the bad apple has started to spoil the bunch, and you realize you should have fired that person long ago. So hire slow, and fire fast."

Ali's advice for entrepreneurs interested in starting a company from the ground up:

1. **"Stick with what you know.** Play to your strengths and delegate your weaknesses. You need to refine assets and make them work for you, and get help in the other areas. You'll have a much better chance of success if you are passionate about what you're doing, so make sure what you're doing and where you're going feels good to you.

2. **Work your numbers.** It blows me away when people start businesses without looking at their market or finding out what their competition is charging. Get on Google, talk with others in the industry, and do your research. Work your numbers and make sure you're going to make money; after all, the purpose of a business is to make a profit! It's noble to want to change the world, but you have to do your homework and make sure you're going to make some money, too.

(continued)

(continued)

3. **Remember: Your marketing is more important than your mastery.** You can be the best at what you do, have the best product, best service, and best employees—but if you don't know how to get the word out, get the right people's attention, and get them to buy, you will never get ahead."

How having a Big Vision has played a part in Ali's success: "I never had a big vision in the beginning. When I started working for myself, my goal was simply to not have to report to a boss. I wanted to make what I made at my last job—which was like 45 grand a year—and I wanted to work from home in my jammies. So that was my Big Vision.

"But every time I had the courage to go another step further, the next vision would appear—and then the next. You have to be open and keep moving forward, creating what you're creating and stepping into your highest level of ability—and the vision will appear. My vision now is huge. I work with women all over the world, helping them both grow personally and create and grow businesses—from women here in America to women in developing countries. I never saw that back then. I just wanted to pay my rent. And that's okay.

How Ali defines success: "Success is whatever you want it to be; it's different for everyone. You need to do what makes you happy, what feels good, and be able to meet your own needs. You need to put food in your mouth and a roof over your head, and take care of yourself and your family. After that, it's really up to you."

The Best of Both Worlds

So which is it then? Are employees the key to time leverage—and therefore the best thing ever—or are they potential nightmares that will drain your wallet and your energy? The reality lies somewhere in the middle. The majority of companies with employees have some great team members, while others are not so great. There will always be good with the bad, and both are simply part of the reality of running a company with employees. But what if there was a way to enjoy the benefits of employees while eliminating many of the drawbacks? What if you could have the best of both worlds? Well, you can—through the use of outsourcing.

The term *outsourcing* gets a bad rap at times, because some people consider it to be synonymous with sending jobs to another country. But the *out* in outsourcing simply means outside your company, not necessarily outside your country—or even outside your city. Outsourcing is a great way to find people to work for you without having to put them on your company's payroll. This concept is worth taking a closer look for just about any business.

Any entrepreneur who is considering outsourcing should be aware that there are many advantages as well as a few drawbacks to outsourced help. We'll take a look at both of these, but let's get the obvious out of the way first. There are clearly some businesses for which employees are necessary. For example, if you have a restaurant, you can't outsource your waitstaff or your dishwasher. On the other hand, it's definitely an option to outsource your bookkeeping and marketing. So although you can't outsource all jobs, almost every business has at least one position that can be turned over to a nonemployee worker. Outsourcing is therefore an important concept to look at, regardless of your industry or business stage. Consider the following advantages to outsourcing workers.

You Can Use Them as You Need Them

Your need for help might not be consistent, especially when you are first starting out. You might need 40 hours' worth of work done one week, and might not need any extra help at all the next. Or, perhaps your company takes on big projects that call for a lot of extra work for short periods with gaps in between. In these cases, hiring permanent employees can end up costing you a lot of money you can't afford. When you hire employees, even on a part-time basis, they expect their employment to be somewhat steady, regardless of whether business is steady or not. On the other hand, you generally don't have to commit to any specific number of hours or guaranteed length of time when you outsource work. You can engage these individuals—from virtual assistants to graphic designers—as needed, and as your budget permits.

They're Easier to Manage

In general, you are dealing with independent people when you work with freelancers or other outsourced employees. They are self-employed individuals running a business, just like you. So you are often dealing with a person who has more of a company owner mentality than an employee mentality. That's not to say that you won't ever have issues with an outsourced worker; however, their general approach to work is often what would be ideal for someone doing a job for your company.

They're Easier to Dismiss

Whether an outsourced worker isn't performing up to your expectations, or you no longer need their services, it's much easier to release them than it is to fire or lay off an employee.

When you outsource, you are dealing with independent contractors who can be released with or without cause at any time. You might have a contract with specific stipulations for this, but you won't be tied to labor laws in which you have no say.

They're Cost-Effective

Typically, when you hire an employee, they actually cost you about one and a half times their hourly wage due to all of the expenses we mentioned earlier that are associated with hiring staff. However, you pay an outsourced worker an agreed-on rate—and that's it. The only additional expense you might have is the cost of an occasional envelope and stamp to mail their checks.

There's Less Paperwork Involved

Not only will outsourced workers save you money in the ways mentioned earlier, they will save you time and expense in the paperwork department as well. You have to register U.S. employees with the state and file quarterly payroll tax forms, deal with employment eligibility verification, get a W-4 from them at the beginning of the year, and issue a W-2 every January. You also have to tackle all that benefits paperwork if you offer health care and other perks, and conduct performance reviews at least once a year. Outsourced workers merely require that you collect a W-9 when they come on board and issue a 1099 at the end of the year—and that's about it!

You Don't Have to Make a Long-Term Financial Commitment

Many entrepreneurs who are starting out in business seek financing, in part, to be able to hire employees. Hiring is clearly a substantial financial commitment. Although you don't generally sign employees on for any guaranteed amount of time, you do create a position that's usually a permanent addition to your expense column. No one likes letting employees go, and you certainly don't ever want to be in a position of *not* being able to meet payroll obligations. Outsourcing allows you to hire workers not only as you need them, but as you can afford them. Outsourced help usually doesn't obligate you financially to any set dollar amount or period of time—something that's clear in the workers' minds. Outsourced employees simply don't expect a long-term obligation, and most employees do.

As you might have guessed by now, our recommendation leans heavily toward outsourcing versus hiring. The advantages are hard to deny, and our experience backs up our belief that outsourcing is a tremendous concept. However, there are certain drawbacks to outsourced workers that you must think about as well. We want to provide a complete picture of the outsourcing model, so the following are some disadvantages to consider.

You Have Less Control Over Them

You can reasonably expect any employee you hire to be at work during specific hours of the day, and you can dictate exactly how you want them to perform the job. Although you are able to provide guidelines and deadlines to outsourced workers, you have to be careful about setting specific parameters around the work to be done. Tax laws make it clear that you cannot just call someone a subcontractor but then treat them like an employee. This often means that you must give them more leeway than you would an employee when it comes to how and when they work.

They're Not Always Readily Available

This point ties in with the one above. Although you know that you can find an employee at his or her desk at 9 AM to work on an emergency project for a big new client, your outsourced worker might have other commitments to attend to and not be available as needed. As Ali Brown mentioned in the case study previously, there were times when she was disappointed to hear that her outsourced employees were working on projects other than her own. However, this was completely within their rights. Depending on the nature of your business, this might not be an issue. However, if you often have last-minute work that needs to be done, you might run into some challenges with outsourced workers.

They Experience Less Emotional Buy-In

Employees often develop a certain amount of company pride and emotional attachment to the organization for which they work. In time, employees can become very loyal to their employers—which is not often the case with outsourced workers. Chances are that your company is one of several for whom they perform work, and although they might feel a certain level of loyalty to you, you are a client—not a boss. The client-outsourcer relationship almost always offers less of an emotional connection than the employer-employee relationship does. Although this doesn't always translate into a disadvantage, outsourced workers' business mentality will often dictate that they work with the clients who pay the best. On the other hand, there are employees who will not leave their job for a higher paying job out of loyalty to their employer.

They Often Work from Home

Many outsourced workers work from home, and many do so successfully. However, this scenario can come with quite a few distractions, and this might become a serious issue depending on the tasks you need done. For example, if you hire a virtual assistant to return phone calls and your clients hear kids yelling and dogs barking in the background, your company will appear unprofessional, and you could lose business.

There are advantages and disadvantages to outsourcing work, and it is important to consider both before making a decision. Outsourcing has been a vital part of our businesses, and we highly recommend using this option whenever possible. If you plan to bring on outsourced help, there are some simple guidelines you can follow to make sure you get the best results.

How to Find the Best Outsourced Workers

When you're considering turning over a portion of your company's work to an outside individual or company, the first step is to determine exactly what you need done and what you hope to accomplish. Make your expectations absolutely clear for the person or company you plan to find. How much work do you have for them? What performance standards and deadlines will you need them to meet? What are you prepared to pay? Just as you would create a job description to fill an employee position, you must do the same for an outsourced position. Just be sure to keep in mind the legal constraints that exist with subcontracted workers.

Once you have a good idea about your needs and how an outsourced worker can fill them, the next step is to research your options for finding someone. There are several virtual assistant and outsourcing databases available that allow you to browse through résumés posted by workers, or create an ad for workers to find you. (We've included some of these databases in the Resources section at the back of the book.) There are also companies that employ various types of workers; you hire the company as a subcontractor, while they provide their employees to perform work for you. Another option is to simply put an ad on a job board, like Craigslist, or use social media to find individuals in your networks that are looking for work.

Regardless of where you find your outsourced help, be sure to conduct thorough research, including interviewing workers and talking with references. If you have taken the time to define exactly what you are looking for in a worker, it will be easy to figure out if a given candidate will fill your needs. This takes some extra time in the beginning, but it will pay off in the long run.

When you have found a worker or company that you feel will fit your needs, the last step in the selection process is to execute an outsourcing agreement. Outsourcing providers will have standard agreements, but individuals might not. Either way, be sure that any agreement you sign protects your interests and spells out all the specifics of the work to be performed, quality and time standards, compensation, and the terms under which you or the worker can end the agreement. You are in the driver's seat here, as there is a lot of competition for work in the outsourcing market. On the other hand, you get what you pay for, so be sure that your final agreement is fair for all parties.

As an internationally recognized expert on outsourcing, there is no one better to provide further insights on the topic than Daven Michaels, our next Entrepreneurial Profile.

Entrepreneurial Profile: Daven Michaels of 123Employee.com

Daven Michaels, entrepreneur since the age of 15, has been labeled the "Super Entrepreneur" by the media and his colleagues. Daven has found success in both the designer clothing retail industry and in electronic music live event promotion. He has produced events for crowds as large as 20,000 people, which led to an award-winning career as a music and television producer. Daven is the author of the book, *Outsource This!* and founder and CEO of 123Employee.com, a company with more than 350 virtual employees that makes outsourcing affordable to all businesses, regardless of size.

What Daven sees as the advantages of outsourcing versus hiring: "There are many upsides to outsourcing versus hiring. There are so many hidden expenses when it comes to hiring: you have to take care of rent, a desk, a chair, a computer, a telephone, long distance, taxes, insurance—the list goes on and on. This can generally equate to receiving an extra employee for free.

"Also, a relevant question to ask is: Does business go straight up on a steady incline? The answer is no. Business goes up and down, and so it's nice to have a solution that's scalable on demand. When you're outsourcing, you can hire a team as you begin to grow; if things get lean, you can let people go; if things begin to expand again, you can bring people back on.

"In addition to that, it's nice to have people working in a different location from where you're headquartered.

It can be a bit of a challenge at first, because it's often easier to train people one-on-one, and in person. But individuals in a remote location are forced to become self-starters, and to think for themselves rather than bug you continuously with questions that they really can figure out on their own. And not having employees in your office gives you the freedom to go out and do the things you want to do; you can go on vacation for a month and not worry about who's minding the shop. You run a lighter, less-expensive business, too."

What Daven sees as the downsides to outsourced workers, and how to overcome them: "The downsides usually involve miscommunications and flaws in the training system. There is a very simple, effective, and easy way to train people well all the time, and it involves using Camtasia or screen capture videos. It is the cleanest, absolute, bar-none best way to train people. The second best would be to give them written training materials or training videos, but the best way is through screen capture videos. You can literally sit at your computer, doing all the moves on your screen, while recording a voiceover at the same time, for instructions, and so forth.

"The first advantage of this is that your training is consistent; every employee gets trained in exactly the same way. You also want to use a firm with happy employees. We have a very low attrition rate at 123Employee; however, if your firm has a high attrition rate, it can be easier if you have these videos in place to train new employees.

"Training is a necessary evil in business. The odds are that you're the trainer if you're an entrepreneur, and it

(*continued*)

(*continued*)

can be time-consuming. Of course, if you train somebody for an hour and they're with you for years, it can be worth hundreds of hours, but that unfortunately is not always the case. That's why having these videos in place just makes your life a billion times easier."

Considerations to keep in mind when choosing outsourced workers: "Any issues we have always have to do with managing expectations. So we've learned that you have to be very straightforward about what you want. You have to make your expectations clear during the interview process and ask those questions to make sure the employee can handle what you want done.

"I also believe that it's important to spend at least 60 days in the training process; therefore, you don't want to make any judgments for the first 60 days. It always takes time for a new employee to get the hang of their employer's needs, and it takes some time for the employer to get used to the employee as well. So get to know each other; it's taking a step backward to take two steps forward."

Daven's advice for entrepreneurs interested in starting a company from the ground up: "Now more than ever, you can start a business for very little money, because you can do it on the Web. But so many businesses fail because they're either undercapitalized or they don't have a plan. So my advice is to have a plan. A plan provides you with a roadmap to follow. Without one, you have no course of action, so the key is to have a plan and then tweak it every six months or so."

How having a Big Vision has played a part in Davon's success: "I've been an entrepreneur for nearly 30 years, and I've had an entrepreneur's mind-set for most of that time. It's only been the last several years where I've moved on to thinking with a bigger business mentality. I think a lot of that stemmed from hanging out with people who were considerably more successful than I was and who were making considerably more money than I was. That really helped me to see business in a different way—to learn about capital markets; how to bring funding into a business; how to take a business to the next level and expand rapidly.

"I think the key is to surround yourself with people who are way beyond your level of success, because you'll learn the secrets that only they know. People will generally be very happy to share those secrets, but you've just got to be around them and spend time with them. That has been the key to my own big vision for success."

How Daven defines success: "I define success as having a ton of money in the bank, a lot of passive income through real estate or business investments, and the freedom to do what I want to do. I love to travel all over the world, and I want to keep that going. So to not have to worry about money and be able to travel and do whatever I want to do means success to me."

5

Laser-Sighted Marketing through Social Media

Everyone is connected. Connect your business to everyone.
—Mitch Joel, author, social media expert

Marketing has been a passion of ours since we started our first business. We've always had an inherent awareness that the key to making any business truly successful lies in the marketing behind it. Many people will tell you that all the marketing you need can come from word of mouth. They claim that if you provide the best product or service, listen to your customers' needs and wants, and offer them fantastic service at every turn, their praise will take you as far as you could ever want to go. Word of mouth can have tremendous power, and it makes a lot of sense to optimize all aspects of your company to maximize word-of-mouth marketing. It is true; after all, that little is more compelling than a trusted friend's recommendation when it comes to making a buying decision.

But there is a reason why established, instantly recognized companies—such as McDonald's, Walmart, and Microsoft—continue to spend millions of dollars annually on marketing, even though people are already talking about them consistently. Word of mouth can only take you so far. For example, it might do the trick if you run a mom-and-pop operation in a small town and have no desire to grow beyond your current market. On the other hand, if you have visions of growing your business beyond limits—of taking your company from average to extraordinary and becoming a true entrepreneurial success story—then word of mouth alone isn't going to cut it.

To realize this kind of success, you need to get the word out, and do it in a big way. Your goal should be to have virtually every person within your target market hear of your company, know what you do, and know exactly why it makes sense to choose you over your competition. Will you ever accomplish the objective of reaching *everyone*? Unless your target market is extremely narrow, probably not. But as long as you're always striving for it, you'll be headed in the right direction.

Marketing is not something you "accomplish"; you'll never be "done" marketing. It is a continuous process that never looks exactly the same for long. It changes as your business changes, and, more importantly, as your customers' needs and expectations change. Just as you must remain flexible in your business plans, your offerings, and other aspects of your business, you must also have a marketing plan that's fluid enough to adapt to the shifting world around you.

Although remaining flexible is important, it is also critical that your marketing activities are laser-focused. That simply means that you take advantage of every marketing effort to ensure that you're reaching the right people, in the right way, every time. In other words, you can't just use a shotgun approach. Failing to execute your marketing efforts in a focused manner will only cause you to waste time and money, and end up frustrated and disappointed. It has become easier than ever as marketing has evolved into the Internet age to focus your efforts and ensure that you are reaching those people—and *only* those people—who want exactly what you have to offer. The days of throwing mud at the wall in hopes that some will stick are in the past—and the age of laser-sighted marketing is here.

To illustrate what we're talking about, think about the limited options traditional marketing offered not long ago. The choices were basically TV, print (newspapers and magazines), radio, direct mail, and various *guerilla marketing* techniques. Although each of these media granted you the ability to target your message to some extent, you were greatly limited in terms of the degree to which you could focus just on your potential buyers.

For example, let's say that your ideal target market is single mothers, age 25 to 40, and you want to reach them through radio advertising. You look at the ratings for the stations you're considering, and you choose the one that has the largest share of that audience. Then you make an ad buy and cross your fingers. The problem with this scenario is that you don't *really* know that your target buyer is listening when the station is playing your message—and you know for sure that you're paying for your message to be played to a sizable number of people who really don't care. Consequently, you have to spend a lot of money to broadcast your ad frequently enough to ensure that a good number of your potential customers hear it. That's why we call it a shotgun approach. You have to spread your message out over a much larger target than necessary, in hopes that you just might occasionally hit your desired target.

Now take that same scenario and apply it to advertising on Facebook. For a much smaller investment, you can target single mothers between 25 and 40, and you can narrow it down much more if you want. Is your ideal customer into reading, snowboarding, or gardening? You can pursue those criteria. Does your product or service play better to conservatives than liberals? Then target them, too. And the best part is that rather than blasting your message to everyone in hopes that your potential customers will see it, your ad will only be visible to those who meet your criteria and obviously, only when they're there to see it. If everyone turned their radios off for a day, you'd still be paying for your ads to go out; however, most paid online advertising models only have you pay when someone actually sees or interacts with your ad. Additionally, you can control your spending by specifying exactly how many impressions you're willing to pay for. That's laser-sighted marketing—and you don't have to be a marketing genius to recognize its power.

The Magic of Social Media Marketing

Our experience has shown that the best way to accomplish highly focused marketing is by using social media. To say that social media has changed the way businesses communicate and market themselves is a complete understatement. It's no secret that social networking sites like Twitter, YouTube, Facebook, and LinkedIn, and bookmarking sites like StumbleUpon and Digg are immensely popular and can be effective tools in any entrepreneur's marketing arsenal. With more than 600 million users, Facebook has a population larger than the United States or the entire European Union. So it's no wonder that even business owners who would not otherwise consider themselves early adopters have flocked to these sites to get a piece of the social media marketing pie.

The fact that so many consumers of almost every conceivable demographic can be found and targeted on these sites—coupled with the reality that much of it can be done at relatively low cost—makes social media marketing somewhat of a no-brainer for most every business. Still, it can be a bit of a mystery exactly how to use these tools most effectively for many entrepreneurs not familiar with social media sites. This might be the reason why so many companies still have not jumped on this massive trend that can go nowhere but up. Through firsthand conversations and in comments on our blogs, we've often interacted with entrepreneurs who suggest that social media marketing doesn't work for their business, or that they just don't have time to learn and manage this marketing medium.

Anyone who is reluctant to wade into the social media waters—for whatever reason—should realize something, however: social media marketing isn't optional. It's a medium through which you can present your offerings to literally *millions* of targeted leads, manage your customer feedback, build relationships with your customers, colleagues, and industry experts, and monitor your entire brand. To dismiss such a powerful tool is simply a foolish business decision—something that's especially true when you consider that the cost to accomplish all this can be low when compared to just about any other form of marketing.

Much of how you can best take advantage of social media has to do with your company's specific needs and goals. What you offer, how you offer it, and who you're trying to reach will all play a part in your approach to social media marketing. However, these factors should play no part in whether you actually use social media to market your company. Every product, from diapers to bulldozers, and every service, from law to scuba classes, can find an audience on social media. Whether your target audience is made up of high school students, doctors, city planners, or retired airline pilots, you'll find plenty of them through social media—so don't make the mistake of dismissing this incredibly valuable marketing tool.

One entrepreneur who has taken social media to its limits is Gary Vaynerchuk. We're pleased to present Gary as our next Entrepreneurial Profile.

Entrepreneurial Profile: Gary Vaynerchuk of Wine Library TV

Gary Vaynerchuk is one of those guys who is known by millions of people for many different reasons. If you are into wine, you probably know Gary from Wine Library TV. If you've been on the hunt for angel investors for the next big thing, there's a good chance someone has mentioned his name to you. And if you've explored the world of social media at all, you have almost certainly run across the name Gary Vaynerchuk (or @garyvee). Gary has taken personal branding to a whole new level, and he has harnessed the power of social media to do so.

Through his books, keynote addresses, videos, and blogs, Gary is widely known as one of the foremost experts on social media marketing today. In addition to having an army of loyal social media fans on various networks, Gary is sought after as a speaker, commentator, and coach to major brands on all things social media.

What Gary thinks about entrepreneurs who choose not to use social media marketing: "I really think that it's tremendous, because it means that there are more pieces of the pie left over for the people like me who actually see the business value in it. At the highest level, I'm thrilled by it. At a 'trying to help out others' level, I think there's some validity, since it's still early and hard to measure. People are not very good at understanding what they can't see. I think emotionally intelligent entrepreneurs have a dramatically bigger awareness of what's actually happening in comparison to more numbers-driven entrepreneurs. Emotional IQ defines the early adopters in this, and overall IQ always eventually catches up to the initial front runners."

The mistakes Gary made early on in social media: "I'm not good at processing what I don't do well, which is probably the foundation of my success. I don't really harp on it or pay attention to it. With that being said, I would say that I did leave an enormous amount of community on the table by not using YouTube instead of Viddler. I wouldn't really say I would do anything different—because YouTube might have led to a different opportunity that would have obviously been interesting—but it could have led me down a path that's different from the place I'm in today. On paper—and in the way that someone would normally process the question of what they would do differently—I would say that my mistake was failing to use YouTube as the core community building driver in the early days of Wine Library TV. However, I wouldn't say I would do it differently. I do feel that my community would be bigger, because YouTube gives a lot of 'by accident' business. However, Conan O'Brien found me through Viddler—so what does that mean?"

Gary's take on what social media marketing does and does not replace: "I don't think social media actually replaces anything because it's such a new genre. It doesn't replace television, print, radio, or anything that way. The way I view social media—and this is such a vague term/ word since everyone translates *social media* to mean

(*continued*)

(*continued*)

something different—is as a reactionary tool. I don't think there's ever been a reactionary tool on the Internet. To me, this has many more customer service and lifetime value marketing initiative themes—more than just driving a message home. I don't think it replaces a lot of the push platforms I mentioned earlier (television, print, radio). I think it replaces something that maybe doesn't exist yet. At the very least, it replaces call centers."

Gary's advice for entrepreneurs interested in starting a company from the ground up: "Be very aware that you are not capable of being 'half pregnant' when starting a business—meaning you have to literally be 'all in.' Somebody else will be all in, and they will beat you. If you're interested in work/life balance in the first 36 months of starting your own business, you will lose."

How having a Big Vision has played a part in Gary's success: "I don't understand anything other than having a big vision. I think it's the core of my success, because I never make short-term decisions. I base everything I do on what I want to happen 20, 30, 40 years from now. It keeps me very grounded while still reaching for the stars."

How Gary defines success: "The real answer is what I'm doing now—doing whatever I want, whenever I want, however I want. The flexibility to do what I want to do for a living and be happy when I wake up is 100 percent success."

Four Keys to Social Media Marketing Success

When it comes to planning for success in social media marketing, some of how you approach it will, as we mentioned, depend on your business. There are some universal lessons to be learned though, and we've presented them here to help you make the most of your social media efforts.

1. Create a Strategic Plan

Small business owners make a plan for nearly every other aspect of their companies, but few actually create a written plan for social media. Yet without one, they're more likely to give up all together because they feel like they're spinning their wheels.

As with all areas of your business, you want to approach social media marketing strategically. If you fail to move forward with a well-defined plan of attack, you won't get the results you want, and you might even do more harm than good. Just as people judge your company based on your Web site's level of professionalism and quality, your potential customers will also judge your brand based on how you handle your social media efforts. If you take a haphazard approach, people just might get the impression that you apply that low degree of focus to all areas of your business. You need to have an effective social media strategy; here's how to build it:

Determine Objectives It is important to know exactly what you want your social media marketing to accomplish before you begin. Many people jump into this realm without having any concrete goals in mind, beyond getting a bunch of "followers." This leads quickly to frustration and, for many, the assumption that social media "doesn't work." Your social media efforts will be more successful when you have clearly defined objectives for your campaigns. Unless you know what you want to accomplish, you won't know if you're on track—and if you don't know if you're on track, you won't be able to make the necessary adjustments to optimize your efforts.

A key element to this piece is setting realistic goals. Social media marketing can be an extremely effective way to accomplish many great things, but you won't achieve instant fame overnight—or without consistent effort. That is why it's best to look six months to a year in the future when setting time frames for your goals. You might have some short-term goals that will lead you to those more distant objectives, but it's important to be realistic and know that you aren't likely to see a significant impact in your business right away.

Common social media marketing objectives include increasing Web site traffic, monitoring or improving your company's reputation, building brand awareness, and increasing sales. Let's take a look at each of these in more detail.

Increasing Web Traffic   Used in conjunction with your search engine optimization efforts, social media has the potential to boost your Web site traffic significantly over time. Once you've developed solid relationships within social media with people who trust you, they'll gladly click through from your social media posts to your Web site. Additionally, when you perform just about any Google search these days, there's a decent chance a tweet will show up as one of the top results. This allows even those outside your network to find your company through your social media efforts.

Again, you won't see increased traffic overnight, but it's completely realistic to expect to increase your traffic through social media in the long term. Set a benchmark, then monitor and tweak it over time as you start to see results.

Monitoring or Improving Reputation Social media is a great way to monitor exactly what people are saying about you—if anything at all. It might seem strange to some that people post every mundane detail of their lives on social media, but this can be great news for a business—or a disaster. If someone just had the best lunch ever at your restaurant, they're going to shout it out to their network. On the other hand, if the service was lousy, that's going to hit the social media sites as well.

We all want people to spread the word about our companies. And although some owners claim that any exposure is good exposure, we really want people to say positive things. Not-so-good news can sting a little; however, the great thing about social media is that it lets you know about it more quickly than any previous methods. When people's only avenues to vent were to chat on the phone with their friends or spout off over dinner, you had no way of knowing what people were saying about your company. Now, you can see the good, the bad, and the ugly, and respond appropriately. Your goals in this area might not be as measurable as some other areas, but there is real value in the ability to monitor your reputation. It's therefore an extremely important part of your social media strategy.

Building Brand Awareness Getting the word out about your brand is a big part of any marketing effort, and social media marketing is no exception. These tools give you the ability to create an authentic brand personality. Whether you want people to see your company as the ultraprofessional, trusted financial services provider, or the hip, quirky T-shirt maker, an effective social media marketing strategy can communicate exactly who you are and what you stand for.

This is another of those objectives that might be difficult to measure in terms of numbers, but that you can evaluate in an abstract way. The crowd that is following your social media activities—and the way in which they are interacting with and talking about your brand—will tell you if you're on the right track and building the right kind of brand awareness.

Increasing Sales   Well, this is what it's all about, isn't it? Any marketing plan should be aimed at increasing sales, and the great thing about this objective is that it is absolutely measurable in real numbers. There are a number of ways you can track where your sales are coming from—campaign-specific landing pages, click tracking, and coupon codes are just a few. You're probably using these tools or something like them anyway, so it's a cinch to apply them to your social media marketing campaigns. Words of caution apply: Don't expect overnight results; stay consistent; and stay focused.

Get to Know Your Audience   A primary concern when you create any marketing plan, social media-based or otherwise, is to define your target audience. Create a profile of who your potential buyers are, where to find them, and what they like and don't like to help you to determine where and how to market to them. The profile you build should answer these questions:

Who are they?
- How old are they?
- What is their income level?
- What is their education level?
- Are they parents?
- Are they married or single?
- Are they men, women, or both?
- What ethnicity are they?

Where are they?

- Do they live in a specific geographic area (certain city, country, region, etc.)?
- Are they members of specific groups, networks, or associations?
- Are they frequent visitors of specific Web sites or types of sites?
- Do they communicate primarily through mobile, e-mail, or Twitter, Facebook, and so on?

What are their likes and dislikes?

- What are their preferences?
- What do they dislike or have a problem with?
- What are they looking for?
- What are they talking about or complaining about?
- What do they spend their money on?

There are other questions you can ask to narrow down your target audience, and the right questions will depend somewhat on the industry you're in. But you should at least know the answers to the above questions to build an effective buyer profile.

Know Your Competition   In addition to your target audience, you also need to know your competition—regardless of the kind of marketing plan you create. You researched your competition as you planned your company, and now you have a good idea of your competitive advantages, as well as your competition's tactics. This step will require you to apply that same research approach to these organizations' social media marketing presence. Which networks and sites do they use? Who is following, "liking," or "friending" them? And most importantly, what are people saying about them and to them? Answering these questions will help you to devise a plan that both addresses your mutual target audience and capitalizes on your competitors' shortcomings.

Social media is just as useful for monitoring your competition as it is for monitoring your own brand. Don't just do the initial research to build your social media marketing plan—continually keep an eye on your competitors to maintain a competitive advantage and quickly respond to your market's needs.

Create a Content Strategy You now know enough about your audience and competition to develop a content strategy. Social media is all about connecting with people, and this step will help you to create content that captures and keeps your target market's attention. It will speak directly to them in a way that will create a connection. Come up with some ideas for content that will resonate with the target audience profile you created. Some suggestions are:

- **Solve a problem:** Based on your audience's likes and dislikes, provide a solution to problems they have expressed.

- **Answer a question:** Look at their discussions and answer their most commonly asked questions.

- **Teach them something:** Think about how you can help your target market do things faster, better, or more efficiently.

- **Provide timely, relevant information:** Take a look at the headlines. What are people talking about that is significant to your market?

- **Turn them on to new ideas or products:** Recommend a product, service, person, or company that they might not already know about.

Determine Networks   Next, you want to determine which Web sites your target audience is using most. The big three are Facebook, Twitter, and LinkedIn. Although many people are on all these networks and more, your audience will likely favor one or two. That's not to say you can't use all three in your social media marketing plan, but you might not need to. Perform a search for keywords associated with your industry on each network, and see how much people are talking about your topics. This will give you a good indication of where to place your emphasis. You should also conduct a search for groups on LinkedIn and Facebook. Not only will the number of groups and people in them give you an idea of your industry's popularity on that network, you'll also want to join many of the groups you find.

Target Your Keywords   One great reason to use social media is to build site traffic. People are using social media sites more and more as search engines to find what they're looking for. Part of your plan should be to define the keywords you want to target in your social media efforts, and then direct that traffic from those sites back to your own site by using links in your social media feeds. The Google Keyword Tool is a great way to narrow down the keywords that make sense for your business.

Provide Quality Over Quantity   The concept of quality over quantity applies to many areas of your business, and your social media strategy is no exception. Blasting out a bunch of content that isn't relevant or that doesn't compel your audience to interact with you is not useful, and it can do more harm than good. When you're creating content to post on social media, take the time to really think about what your audience wants, and only post when you have something meaningful to say.

Implement Your Plan   The next step in your social media content strategy is "where the rubber meets the road," so to speak. Putting your plan into action doesn't have to be difficult, as long as you're able to answer some specific questions:

- **Who will be responsible for creating content and maintaining your social media presence?** Many entrepreneurs don't have the time to properly maintain their social media marketing plan, so they delegate the task. That's okay, but remember that this is an important part of your business. Turning this task over to an intern or your teenage niece or nephew will likely not produce the results you want. If you don't have the time or desire to do it yourself or the qualified staff to take it on, consider hiring a third-party provider. There are more than a few great social media marketing companies to choose from, and it doesn't have to cost you a fortune.

- **How often will you post to your social media networks?** Will it be once a day, several times daily, or daily on one network and weekly on another? The answer to this question should not depend on your available time as much as your social media goals. It's a good idea to adjust this as you measure results and amend your strategy.

- **How much time and money are you willing to invest?** If you're not planning to outsource your social media marketing, plan your days to include your social media activities. Also, if you don't intend to handle it yourself, budget for hiring someone internally or from a third-party firm.

Consider all your options for each of these questions and choose the ones that make the most sense for you, your business, and your overall marketing strategy.

2. Create Conversion (Get Them to Buy!)

If one of your objectives for social media is to increase your revenue, then you'll need to plan accordingly. Social media marketing can result in more people buying what you have to offer, which is one reason we advocate it so strongly. Whether you're a blogger looking to increase traffic to your monetized site, a personal coach hoping to bring on more clients, or the owner of a shoe store wanting more "foot" traffic, social media marketing can help you accomplish your goals.

Remember though: Although social media marketing can bring results, the results you see won't be in the form of paying customers unless you work both ends of the social media channel. In other words, your social media strategy can get traffic flowing to your site, but then it's up to you to have measures in place to turn that traffic into cash. The great thing about social media traffic, versus, say, search engine traffic, is that when you do it right, the visitors that come to you through social media will feel as though they know you, and will already trust you. Rather than just being one of 10 million search results, you and your company are members of their community. Even so, just as you optimize your company's site to convert other visitors, you'll need to do the same for your social media traffic. You should take steps such as building an opt-in e-mail list, creating calls to action throughout your site, and following up with current and potential buyers on your list through regular e-mail marketing.

You'll also want to create landing pages on your Web site specific to your social media posts; consider running contests for your social media "fans"; and offer coupons and discounts tailored to your social media audience. The more fun, interesting, or useful you can make your fans' experience, the more likely they are to connect with and buy from you.

3. Measure and Adjust

As with any goals or plans, it is vital to recognize what about your social media strategy is working and what is not, and then adjust accordingly. Your plan is only as good as the results it produces, so keep it flexible enough to respond to the outcome you are seeing. Some measurements to monitor are:

- How many likes, shares, and retweets is your content getting?
- How many comments do you receive on each post?
- How many new followers and friends do you gain, and how many, if any, do you lose on a weekly basis?
- What are people saying about your content? Where is the conversation taking place?
- Which keywords and tags are getting hits and which aren't?
- Which links are being clicked and which aren't?
- Are your trackbacks, pingbacks, and incoming links increasing?
- Is your content resulting in increased traffic—and is your increased traffic resulting in increased dollars?

Social media marketing—like any kind of marketing—is not a "set it and forget it" activity. You must use the answers to the questions above to modify your strategy, and stay on top of your audience's preferences and activities.

4. Follow Best Practices

Many people have been using social media effectively for years and have figured out what works well and what doesn't, and many of them have shared their knowledge freely. The following three points illustrate the most important best practices that are generally accepted for effective social media marketing.

Create Compelling Content   People decide to tune into your social media feeds and content based on the value you deliver. Although it's important to connect on a personal level, you won't attract the attention you're looking for if all you ever tweet about is what you're having for lunch or that you have to take your dog to the vet. The key is to keep your content engaging while delivering your company's message and letting your personality shine through.

Engage   The whole point of social media is that it's *social*, so use it as a way to engage with your customers, readers, users, and so on. Create two-way conversations with your market. Respond when someone connects with you, ask questions, and create a dialogue. Even large corporations like Ford and Starbucks use social media to connect with individual customers, so it's absolutely expected that true entrepreneurs would do the same.

Shut Up and Listen   Remember that while you're creating content and engaging with your audience members no one is going to care about your company until they feel as though they have a personal connection with you. It's therefore vital to focus your efforts on your audience's needs and desires rather than just spouting off information about your products and services. Unlike other advertising mediums where you're talking *at* your customers, social media is about listening to your audience's requests and responding appropriately.

Bonus Tip: Use Social Media Automation Tools Properly

Some estimates claim that more than 80 percent of all tweets are generated by automated Twitter tools, and automated Facebook and LinkedIn posts are growing in popularity as well. Such trends are prompting people to become leery of some types of content. These tools can be great ways to manage your time, but they aren't practical replacements for actually talking to people on the sites. Using a combination of live interaction and social media tools is a great way to balance your time for maximum effectiveness.

One of the most compelling social media marketing success stories we've heard is that of our next Entrepreneurial Profile—Mike Roberts of SpyFu. Here's what he had to say about his effective use of new media.

Entrepreneurial Profile: Mike Roberts of SpyFu.com

Mike Roberts is founder and CEO of Velocityscape, the market leader in Web data extraction products and services. As an entrepreneur since age 11, Mike embodies what it means to be a true self-starter and entrepreneur. As such, he has embraced all forms of technology, including social media marketing, to make a name for himself—and build a great business, too! Through a focused new media approach, Mike and his team have created tremendous buzz for their signature product, SpyFu. The way he has expertly leveraged social media and other new media methods to build his brand and drive traffic to his business is really something to admire, and something from which any budding entrepreneur can learn.

How Mike has used new media marketing to build his company: "SpyFu.com allows you to type in any domain name and see every keyword they've ever bought on Google AdWords. SpyFu Recon Files tell you which articles you should write to rank well in unpaid Google results. So it would be really convenient for me to say that pay per click (PPC) advertising or even search engine optimization (SEO) is the secret to our success. And those things *have* played a role for us—particularly SEO.

"But, our real success has been due to the enormous amount of goodwill we've received from industry bloggers. There have been hundreds of reviews and articles written about SpyFu; those reviews brought inbound links, and from those links came some pretty good SEO. I'd love to

(*continued*)

(*continued*)

say that was all part of some ingenious master plan that I devised long before building the site. Unfortunately, I'm not that smart.

"We did, however, do some things that made it much more likely for people to *want* to write about us.

1. **We did something completely new.** Nothing like it had been done before, and we were the first to do it. That's known as the 'first mover's advantage,' and it's tough to replicate. But if I left it out, I'd be leaving out a big part of why someone would want to write about us.

2. **We had a three- to four-month beta period where we provided all of our material and services completely for free.** It gave people a chance to use it, and a sense of urgency to tell their readers about it.

3. **We built the site from the ground up with a big chunk of functionality that would be free forever.** I think that's really important. Nobody wants to talk about something they have to pay for; they feel like they're selling out, right? But, they'll go to a tradeshow and give a 60-minute presentation on the top five free [whatever]. We've therefore found that it's absolutely critical to make some part of the product permanently free."

"So, here's the equation to remember: Innovative Product + Something Free = Blogger Love."

Mike's take on what social media marketing does and does not replace: "Obviously, I like the Internet. It's pretty awesome. Things like Facebook and YouTube,

Gotowebinar and LivePerson, AdWords and Mailchimp, Twitter and PRWeb extend our reach dramatically. Businesses like mine wouldn't be impossible, but they'd be shaped very differently without them.

"Yet despite the help these sites provide, they're all a pretty shabby replacement to actually meeting your customers in real life. Whether you can expect to make enough sales to justify the cost or not (we can't), I highly recommend buying a booth at an industry tradeshow from time to time—and taking your nonsalespeople. Get drunk with your customers; seriously just find situations in which you can be yourself. You might regret it, you might not. But, nothing can replace the experience of making bad decisions in a new city with people you should be trying to impress.

"I know that kind of sounds like bad advice. But, consider this: When we launched SpyFu U.K. we thought we were being tongue-in-cheek using the word 'bloody' in our launch e-mail. I mean, James Bond says it all the time, right? Turns out, that word is offensive in Britain; so we were basically cursing at 7,500 of our potential customers. That's probably something I could have gleaned from a chat with one English guy over a pint. So, at the end of the night, if you end up vomiting on one *single* customer's shoes, what's the big deal, right? At least you didn't stay home and alienate an entire nation. (For the record, I've never *actually* vomited on a customer's shoes.)"

The mistakes Mike made early on in marketing his business: "Our official customer service policy at SpyFu is 'Don't be a dick.' So, we avoid doing things that other company's do that we think are underhanded and insulting

(*continued*)

(*continued*)

to customers. For example, we hate it when companies make it difficult to cancel something by requiring a phone call or a fax, hiding the cancel button, et cetera. We make it really easy to cancel SpyFu; you can click a button, send us an e-mail, chat with us, tweet it—send an owl, whatever.

"For a long time, I thought that sending someone an e-mail any other time than the day we launch a new product violated this rule. I think that's because of my own bias against e-mail. So, for the first three years, we'd send customers only about one e-mail every two months. It turns out, however, that our customers actually *like* to hear from us. They want to get excited about something 'coming soon.' Product launches are like an experience that they want to share and be the first to know about and tell their friends. They want to hear about tips, new features and cool things we are doing.

"I was pretty surprised by all that. As a result, we now send out about an e-mail a week, and our open rate is actually higher than it was when we were sending them every two months. Of course, engaging customers by e-mail also drives sales.

"It all seems painfully obvious to me now. But, I guess the broader lesson is: marketing to people about something they want to hear about is *not* the same as annoying them."

Mike's advice for entrepreneurs interested in starting a company from the ground up:

1. "**Don't guard your ideas**. I don't care how awesome *you* think your idea is; nobody is going to steal it. It's kind of sad and comforting at the same time. I tried to give away

the idea of SpyFu for three years. But, sharing your idea with anyone who will listen will get you really good feedback and help make it better. Seriously, try giving your ideas away. My first 30 posts on Twitter were product ideas I was sitting on for months. When I have a new one I tweet it @mrspy.

2. **Whatever you do, don't think you have to come up with something totally new**. In fact, if something hasn't been invented yet, it's *most likely* that there isn't a market. Competition is a good thing. Look for a market that's small enough for you to compete, but big enough for you to grow. Fragmented competition is also good.

3. **If you're like me and are only excited when you come up with something completely new and revolutionize an industry, then here's my advice: Trust your ideas, but refine them to the point you can prototype them quickly.** And choose to work on the ones that scale well."

How having a Big Vision has played a part in Mike's success: "The problem in business is never a lack of ideas; the problem is having too many. At any given time, we've got a list of 10 to 20 great products that we *want* to introduce. But because our mission is to *answer the questions people need answered to be profitable in search engine marketing*, we ignore a lot of cool ideas that are not relevant to that mission. And that is the definition of focus: Not doing 'good ideas,' but working on the ones that connect to your organization's goals. So, the vision gives us focus."

How Mike defines success: "An endless cycle of failures that you manage to learn from."

6

From Entrepreneur to Icon

Achieving Expert Status

How can you squander even one more day not taking advantage of the greatest shifts of our generation? How dare you settle for less when the world has made it so easy for you to be remarkable?

—Seth Godin

Becoming a recognized expert in your field is an excellent way to boost your business by adding additional streams of revenue to your current model. Whether through extensive education, years of hands-on experience, or a natural aptitude for a specific area of business (or a combination of all of these things), there are plenty of entrepreneurs who could justifiably be considered experts in their fields, even though many of these experts are not widely recognized as such. In fact, some who *are* considered to be "experts" could actually learn a thing or two from others in the same field who no one has heard of. That's because you don't have to be the most knowledgeable or successful person in your field to be seen as an expert; you just have to do what it takes to become *recognized* as one.

This assertion tends to get many protests from entrepreneurs who have a specific notion of what constitutes an expert. People tend to put experts on a pedestal that sets them apart from us mere mortals. The truth, however, is that they're no different from you or me. In fact, anyone who knows more about a topic than most people can be considered an expert on that topic—and just about everyone knows more about *something* than most people. Experts are simply people who have knowledge about a particular subject and have decided to share that knowledge with the world. What makes us refer to them as experts more than anything else is simply that they call themselves experts and put their expertise out there long enough to cause others to begin using that title for them.

Embracing Your Expertise

It doesn't matter what your area of expertise is—you can turn it into a revenue stream, and even an information empire, if you choose to take it there. Your reach is practically infinite if you use the Internet and rapidly mounting popularity of social media. Regardless of your area of expertise, you have access to millions of people who potentially fit into your target market.

There are more than a billion people online. If you can capture the attention of just a fraction of those looking for more information on your subject of choice, you've found a potential gold mine. Whether you're a seasoned financial planner, a whiz at search engine optimization (SEO), or someone who just loves candle making and everything to do with it, you can bet there are millions of others out there who don't know as much as you do about the subject. This means that there are millions of people who will identify with you, and a portion of those will be willing to spend money to get the inside scoop on your ideas.

Reaching expert status can substantially boost whatever you consider to be your primary business. Plenty of people have made a fortune on books, seminars, speaking engagements, and other "expert-like" activities. Even if you're not interested in selling your expertise in those ways, the sheer marketing power of attaining expert recognition will launch your business to a level few other activities can match.

So how do you either make your expertise your business, or use it to boost your current business? First, the bad news: It's not going to happen overnight. If you're looking for a way to make a quick million, this path will only get you there if you're an already-recognized expert on a wildly popular topic, or a celebrity with an established following. The good news is that with some patience and perseverance, you can turn any area of expertise into an incredible marketing machine or a full-time stand-alone business. And with some outside-the-box thinking and creativity, you can indeed make it a million-dollar enterprise.

If you're still not convinced that you're an expert at something, you might find it helpful to drop the word *expert*. For some, that word has a specific meaning that they just can't seem to equate with who they are. So if that's the case for you, don't get hung up on the word. The bottom line is that if you love to do something, or know how to do something really well, you're an expert. It's as simple as that.

Building Your Information Empire

How do you use what you know and love to have others recognize you as an expert? There are specific steps anyone can take to go from simply being great at what they do to becoming the curator of their own information empire.

Five Steps for Going from Entrepreneur to Icon

It takes time and patience to become a recognized expert, and more than anything, it takes consistent action. Here's what to do if you're up for the challenge:

1. Start Blogging If you're going to establish yourself as an expert, you've got to give people reason to believe that you actually know what you're talking about. There's no easier way to do that than with a blog. Blogging allows you to share your thoughts and knowledge on any topic, without having to spend much money or to convince a publisher or literary agent to take you on. There are many sites and books on how to get started blogging, so we won't go into that here. However, it's important to know that creating a blog is an essential step toward asserting yourself as an expert.

This can seem like an intimidating undertaking for someone who's never written a blog before—but it doesn't have to be. If you know what you're talking about, it's just a matter of transforming that information into written content. One great technique for making blogging easier is to write as though you're talking to an audience of eager listeners. Pretend they can't wait for you to share your expertise with them, and then deliver what they came to hear . . . in writing.

One concern that we hear from new bloggers is that they are reluctant to give their "best stuff" away for free through blog posts. Though this is an understandable concern, plenty of people have blogged for years and then turned around and sold much of that exact same content in book or e-book form—and have done so successfully. The truth is that unless you truly know something that no one else in the world knows, the information is already somewhere on the Internet. Also, different formats appeal to different people. Some people prefer to only read blogs, while others might only skim your blog but will gladly snap up your book. So don't hesitate to really let your knowledge shine, and give "your best stuff" to your readers. They'll appreciate it so much that they'll return to read more, tell their friends about it, and when the time comes, they *will* buy what you have to sell.

2. Market *Yourself* As an expert, you are your own brand. *You* become the product you are promoting, and that product is separate from your primary business. Even though you have a marketing plan for your company, you'll want to create a separate strategy for you as an expert. The marketing you do for your expertise and for your business can feed into one another. In other words, those who find you through your efforts to market yourself will find out about your business, and those who come to you through your primary business marketing channels will learn about you, the expert.

You can apply the laser-sighted marketing techniques from the previous chapter here, and we've also provided some great links in the Resources section toward the back of the book. In addition, a simple Google search will help you find a lot of useful information. Find the best, most current advice, and absorb as much as you can. Learn all you can, but don't let the learning process keep you from taking action on the first step. Launch your blog, start writing, begin creating products, and learn as you go. Unless you already have an established following, you won't get much (or any) traffic to begin with—which is fine. It's no reason to wait; after all, once you do learn how to get traffic, you want to send people to a site with plenty of quality content on it.

Remember as well that even your earliest content can get indexed by search engines and found by visitors looking for that information in the future. It also shows that you've been around for a while; and, there's no way for potential site visitors to know that your older posts heard crickets when they first went live.

3. Create Compelling Content Whether we're talking about your blog posts, your social media content, e-books, video or audio programs, or just your general site content, it's critical to give your audience something that interests them—and leave them wanting more. You might not be the greatest writer, and that's okay. If you look around at some of the most successful blogs out there, you'll see that many of the experts on various topics cannot consider themselves expert *authors*. The idea is to create content that gets your blood pumping. If you're passionate about your topic, your enthusiasm will come across in your writing, videos, and audio content, and that's the most important thing you can communicate to your readers. People are drawn to someone who clearly loves what he or she is doing, and hopefully that's the case with you.

Keep in mind, though, that you'll want to have someone edit your writing if you really struggle with grammar, spelling, and punctuation. You don't have to be Hemingway, but even if the message is strong and compelling, poorly written content can do more harm than good. People will form an opinion about you and your company based on the material you offer, and you don't want potential buyers to think that you're sloppy or unskilled. So although you want to create compelling subject matter, you must be sure that you focus on quality as well.

4. Create Products Using your blog content as a base, begin creating products that people will be willing to purchase. Some examples of this include e-books, audio and video programs, webinars, workshops, and books. It isn't necessary to wait until you have a large following or a flood of site traffic; begin producing content that you can sell immediately. You can generate this content as you build your following. As your traffic numbers grow, you'll receive questions and comments from followers and fans that will give you ideas as to what people want to know, and that will help you direct and refine your paid content.

Research which mediums are right for you and how to use them to produce your material. It's not hard; it's just a matter of learning the ins and outs. If you have some money to invest, you can hire someone to walk you through the process, or even do it all for you. Think of this investment as part of your marketing budget, as the products you create will not only generate their own revenue, they will help to drive people to your other business offerings as well.

That's the great advantage of becoming a recognized expert: You give your primary business a tremendous amount of exposure and credibility. Let's say you own a landscaping company, and you have a competitor whose work and prices are comparable to yours. But unlike your competitor, who relies on a yellow pages ad to acquire new business, you've been on the local news stations' morning shows, written a book, and have established yourself as a landscaping icon. Who do you think everyone is going to want to hire to complete their landscaping projects? You, of course—the icon!

5. Take It to the Next Level Over time, you'll become known as the expert you never knew you were. There are innumerable ways to capitalize on this persona as it grows. Register as an expert to be found by media companies, corporations, and other organizations looking for expert commentators, speakers, or consultants. Let people know through your social media connections, networking activities, and Web site that you are available to speak and consult, either for free or for a fee. Plenty of experts who started out speaking for free to get their names out have ended up commanding tens of thousands of dollars for a single keynote address.

Also consider creating higher-end products to sell—books, multipart CD programs, workshops, seminars, boot camps . . . the list is endless. Once you have firmly established yourself as a recognized, respected expert in your field, you can also set up one-on-one coaching and consulting programs for big bucks. The sky's the limit.

It's easy to get inspired to do this; just look at anyone you consider to be an expert and know that you can do the same in your field as they're doing in theirs. Is it your dream to be on the *Today Show* or *Letterman*? You can be! Or maybe your goal is to be recognized as the go-to person within your professional community; you can achieve that, too. Whatever expert status means to you, you can attain it if you plan for it and follow through.

Regardless of whether you know it or believe it to be true, you *are* an expert on something—and you owe it to the world to share your knowledge with those who want to learn from you. Is it going to be harder than we make it sound? Probably. Will you run into unexpected challenges and obstacles? Absolutely. Welcome to the entrepreneurial world! But remember this: There isn't a success story in the history of the world that doesn't include tales of hard work and overcoming challenges. If anyone anywhere has done it before, so can you. Don't make excuses. Make it your Big Vision, and then make it happen!

Shama Hyder Kabani is an entrepreneur who had a thriving marketing business but was not content to rest there. She set out to become a recognized expert, and it has paid off in big ways for her.

Entrepreneurial Profile: Shama Hyder Kabani of The Marketing Zen Group

In an online world where roughly a million people claim to be social media experts, Shama Hyder Kabani has taken her knowledge and passion for social media marketing to become one of the most sought-after experts in the field. From writing her book, *The Zen of Social Media Marketing*, to speaking at dozens of corporate and industry events, to her appearances in media such as MSNBC, the *Wall Street Journal*, *BusinessWeek*, CBS, and many more, Shama has truly capitalized on her knowledge to achieve expert status.

Shama is also a great example of how becoming a recognized expert can boost your primary business. Her company, The Marketing Zen Group, has become a destination for those looking for advice on all aspects of marketing, and has been featured in print and online publications worldwide. Shama's experience proves that achieving expert status is both attainable and profitable.

Shama's path to expert status: "Well, I certainly didn't plan to become an expert in the traditional sense. My expertise is derived from an academic background. While doing my graduate studies at the University of Texas in Austin, I was very attracted to social media. Twitter had been around for a few months at that time, and was averaging about 5,000 users. In these early days of social media, companies certainly had not seen this area's potential yet. It was mostly early tech adopters and geeks like me who were using social media. I even did my thesis on Twitter because I was fascinated by the rise of people as a new form of media.

(continued)

(*continued*)

"After graduating, I offered my expertise to various consulting firms. I was rejected 18 times by companies who believed that social media was merely a fad. So, I started my own company, at first as a consultant, and then as a full-service digital marketing firm. Within two years, we've grown from just me to 25 employees, and have the pleasure of serving clients from New York to France."

The steps Shama took to become a recognized expert: "In short, I became a rapid content creator and educator. To stand out as an expert in any field, you must do two things: (1) Create content that educates and entertains people; and, (2), always keep learning. To be a good teacher, you must first be an excellent student. Technologies and techniques change by the hour in my field. In order to educate my marketplace, I started a blog, launched a Web TV show, created a newsletter, and started speaking. I took any chance I had to share my knowledge or gain new knowledge."

How Shama's core business has benefited from her becoming a recognized expert: "The following are just a few of the things that my expertise has stimulated in my core business:

- My company, The Marketing Zen Group, grew 400 percent in the last year alone.
- My book, *The Zen of Social Media Marketing*, was picked up by a publisher and has been one of the best sellers in Web marketing. It has also been translated into Greek, Chinese, and Korean.

- Members of the media regularly call on me to comment on technology and business trends.
- I am now an internationally sought speaker, with speaking engagements ranging in locales from Mexico City to Hong Kong.
- My Web TV show, Shama.Tv, was recently listed by *Inc.* magazine as one of the top three video blogs on the Internet.

"I didn't plan for any of this to specifically take place. I just focused on creating useful content, and syndicating it."

What Shama would change if she could do it all over: "I would have started utilizing Web video a lot sooner! I had been blogging for two years when I came across this statistic: 64 percent of people will finish watching up to a 30-minute commercial video clip, versus 24 percent that will finish reading an article. That got me to start my Web TV show at Shama.Tv. Within just three months, one of my videos had been downloaded over 8,000 times. I never had that type of traction with my written blog. I've come to find that to attain expert status, it isn't just the type of content that you create that matters, but how you present it as well."

Shama's advice for entrepreneurs interested in starting a company from the ground up:

1. "**Learn to be an editor at heart.** If you wait for perfection, you will never move ahead. So do your best, get your material out there, and edit, edit, edit!

(*continued*)

(*continued*)

2. **Invest in what matters, and bootstrap where you can.** Spend money on training for yourself and on hiring a good team. Skip the fancy office.

3. **Listen to your marketplace.** When I first started the company, I insisted on only consulting our clients. However, when I truly listened, I realized that they wanted implementation, too. They wanted to be able to hand their Web marketing over, because they didn't have the time to do it themselves or lacked certain in house resources. So, we went from consulting to allowing our clients to outsource their marketing to us. I've never looked back."

How having a Big Vision has played a part in Shama's success: "Even though I never mapped out my success in this particular way, I've always been a fan of having a big vision for the future. I know what I'd like to see on the horizon for myself and the company, but I've never insisted that there is only one road to get there. I've been open to what presents itself to me, and I think that's half the battle."

How Shama defines success: "I don't have a long-term definition of success. I define it in each moment, and each day. Some days, just getting to spend enough time with my family is success to me. If I am at peace with what I am doing—no matter how mundane or glamorous—I consider that to be true success."

7

The Socially Responsible Entrepreneur

It's Not Always about You

The best reason to start an organization is to make meaning; to create a product or service to make the world a better place.

—Guy Kawasaki

A common thread that often runs through conversations with entrepreneurs—especially younger ones—is their desire to make a difference in the world. Indeed, entrepreneurship itself makes a difference. Business owners create jobs, purchase supplies, buy and rent commercial real estate, and help to keep the economy afloat. When unemployment rates are high, the ability to start a business allows many people to make a living, while the jobs that new businesses create aid in easing the unemployment burden. Anyone who becomes an entrepreneur is making a positive contribution in many ways. Some take it a step further, and we encourage every business owner to look seriously at the opportunities that lie in becoming a social entrepreneur.

As recently as 15 years ago, terms like, *renewable, fair trade,* and *sustainability* were considered by many to be the vocabulary of the fringe. The people who uttered these words were referred to by some as *tree huggers* or *granolas,* and many businesspeople were more concerned with making some cold hard cash than with making a difference. That's not to say that the corporate world has always been filled with self-centered individuals. The largest percentage of charitable donations has always come from companies, and many corporations have included "making a difference in the world" as part of their mission for years. Still, the growing emphasis on improving our society and environment as we build our businesses has recently shifted into high gear.

These days, you're almost as likely to catch CEOs talking about corporate or social responsibility as you are to hear them pushing for bottom-line growth. Though it's difficult to pinpoint why this shift has taken place, it might have something to do with the mounting number of young idealists who've started companies over the past decade—many of which have gone on to become huge corporations. Or, it might be because our world is facing unprecedented challenges in so many areas right now. From growing poverty to environmental threats and energy issues, there are plenty of problems that need attention, and a lot of entrepreneurs who want to address them.

Social Entrepreneurship Is True Entrepreneurship

Whatever the reason, social responsibility in business is here now and growing quickly. But what exactly does it mean to be a "socially responsible" entrepreneur? A social entrepreneur is someone who incorporates actions into his or her business model that help to make the world a better place. That doesn't mean that your business has to be about developing green energy technology or selling organic vegetables. Socially responsible entrepreneurs don't necessarily devote their *entire* businesses to furthering social causes. It can simply be about doing what your business does best, and taking factors such as the environment, poverty, or social equality into consideration when making business decisions.

To us, socially responsible entrepreneurship is *true* entrepreneurship. We say that because true entrepreneurs are known for long-term, big-picture thinking. In fact, that's what having a big vision is all about: the ability to look toward the future and picture the end result, then plan for that result and follow through on that plan. So how does that translate into social entrepreneurship? Simply put, social entrepreneurs think more about the long-term, big picture than most other people. Rather than thinking in terms of what they want for themselves right now, they think of what they want for their kids and grandkids when they grow up. They consider the impact their actions will have on future generations. They are concerned with building their businesses and making a profit, but not at the expense of long-term sustainability.

Social entrepreneurs take responsibility for their actions. Good businesspeople—those who tend to be the best leaders and examples to others—have the courage to say, "The buck stops here." They don't pass their responsibilities off to someone else or assume that the next guy will fix the mess they made. Social entrepreneurs recognize the need for everyone to take responsibility for social progress and for the Earth we all share. Simply by making everyday business decisions with the future of the planet and its inhabitants in mind, social entrepreneurs are increasing in ranks and shifting the old business paradigm in a new direction.

In fact, more and more entrepreneurs are focusing their efforts primarily on charitable or world-changing causes, replacing the profit motive altogether. The trend toward starting a business with the sole purpose of helping people in need is growing quickly, and it shows no signs of slowing. Some companies focus on offering low-income entrepreneurs start-up grants or single mothers educational opportunities, while others provide citizens of third-world countries a chance to earn a living by producing products to sell around the world. These social enterprises are often non-profit, and some operate as a for-profit company while committing a percentage of gross profits to the cause they support. Starting this kind of a company is a great way to make a real difference in the world while experiencing the joy, challenges, and triumphs that comes with being an entrepreneur!

For an excellent example of someone who has chosen social entrepreneurship and been very successful, we turn to our next Entrepreneurial Profile, Adam Braun.

Entrepreneurial Profile: Adam Braun
of Pencils of Promise

As a magna cum laude graduate from Brown University, Adam Braun could have taken many paths. He could have had a bright future at a number of corporate firms, or followed his entrepreneurial spirit to create the next big dot-com, consulting firm, or product-based business. Instead, Adam followed a different passion and founded a company that has been called one of the world's most impactful new nonprofits. Pencils of Promise is now one of the fastest growing nonprofits in the country, with more than 250 domestic-based projects being launched by PoP supporters and school-building programs in Laos, Nicaragua, and Guatemala. The company has attracted the attention and support of Nobel Peace Prize winner Archbishop Desmond Tutu, Barbara Walters, and Katie Couric, and has even secured teen pop sensation Justin Bieber as its spokesperson. In creating a dedicated community of more than 100,000 members, PoP has become a leader in social media engagement, sustainable development, youth empowerment, and digital innovation.

How and why Adam became a social entrepreneur: "Most social entrepreneurs, at least those who are driven by passion, don't have much of a choice in the kind of business we start. It feels more like the path chooses us. We have a transformational seed experience.

"I used to want to be an investment banker until I asked a child begging on the streets of India what he wanted most in the world. He asked for a pencil—and from that point forward I simply knew that I was meant to create a certain type of organization. I've never hoped that Pencils of Promise would become a leader in the global education space and build hundreds of schools for children in need of education; I simply *know* that it's bound to happen. PoP is only at the start of its long-term trajectory, but the only way your idea will succeed is if you believe with that level of relentless conviction that it will. The bonus is that if there's a social mission at its core, which allows you to mobilize other passionate people to support that vision."

How Adam had the idea for Pencils of Promise (PoP):
"After my encounter with the child in India, I felt a sense of promise that came in handing out that first pencil. This led my sharing thousands more while backpacking through 50-plus countries. During these travels, I consistently received advice from locals to one day start an international nonprofit. They felt that it should be led by a local staff from within each country, require village participation in each school, and be deeply supported while training and tracking each student to ensure their success.

"I founded Pencils of Promise in October 2008 with just $25 and the hopes of building one school in Laos by engaging other people who believed in these same principles—in particular, the promise of youth. Others' reactions to the PoP approach of nonprofit idealism and for-profit business accountability soon became so encouraging I left my job at a leading consulting firm, Bain & Company, to work exclusively on realizing the PoP dream—which has now expanded to more than 20 schools in Laos, Nicaragua, and Guatemala."

(continued)

(*continued*)

Adam's advice for entrepreneurs who want to be social entrepreneurs: "I've got a lot of advice for social entrepreneurs. Here are some key things to keep in mind:

- **Only pursue a founding concept that you deeply believe will work.** You're going to have to break down countless walls and overcome tremendous obstacles, but the single most powerful asset that you will have is your personal belief in your idea.

- **You cannot bring your vision to fruition alone; you need to invest lots of time up front finding and vetting your core leadership team.** Only with their help will you succeed, so treat them with the respect and value they deserve.

- **It's important to balance overt confidence in your idea with personal humility.** While no one wants to get behind an idea that even the founder doesn't support, they also don't want to encourage someone who cannot admit when they're wrong. Striking that balance between confidence and humility can make or break a lot of social entrepreneurs.

- **Embrace the late, sleepless nights.** It's during the dreaming hour when you're removed from the rest of the world that the magic happens, and when you form earth-shaking ideas.

- **Surround yourself with a combination of experience and youth.** You'll need the experienced individual to help guide the organization, but it's the younger crowd that will power the engine by providing inspiration and unseen ideas."

How having a Big Vision has played a part in Adam's success: "Having vision is essential. The Big Vision is not stagnant; it starts with a seed idea that you're constantly chasing, but it evolves as you get closer to it. It will most likely always stay just out of reach, because the more you learn, the better you want to be in your space. If you've attained your Big Vision, then you've probably worked yourself out of a job. In the case of my field—global education—there are 75 million children in the world without access to education, so I guess I'm going to be working for a very, very long time."

How Adam defines success: "I define success in terms of fulfillment and your influential ability to spread positivity."

Sustainability Is the New Bottom Line

Although there is no universally accepted definition of "sustainability," most people would agree that the concept has to do with ensuring that we—as a society, planet, and so forth—are at least as well off at any point in the future as we are today. If an action we take today somehow harms a system, society, species, or resource in the future, then that action is not sustainable. In other words, if we continue to take that action, then eventually these elements will be damaged or depleted irreparably.

With that definition in mind, we have come to the point where most serious businesspeople realize that it is not a question of *whether* sustainable business practices are necessary; it is only a question of *how* we effectively and profitably implement sustainability in our businesses. The sustainability "movement" is not simply a fad or passing trend, nor is it merely a liberal or environmentalist agenda. It is a widespread realization that we literally have no other choice. If we want to be able to pass our companies down to future generations, we must make sure that the way we conduct business now supports the ability for those future generations to continue building on what we started.

Sustainable business is especially exciting, because it can actually save money and even increase revenue in a number of ways. Many organizations have found that sustainable changes—ranging from switching to more energy-efficient lightbulbs in their offices to reducing their products' packaging material—don't just help to reduce waste and conserve resources, they can also enhance their bottom lines as well. Likewise, as awareness of fair trade labor matters and other social concerns grow and these become more important issues to a rapidly expanding audience, support of those causes becomes more important from a public relations standpoint. It would be nice to think that all companies always make choices based on doing the right thing. However, when that isn't the case, the prospect of a YouTube video of a Malaysian sweatshop with a company's logo all over it might make a company think twice about their choices.

Whatever the motive may be—to make the world a better place, improve profitability, or just to look good to potential buyers—social entrepreneurship just makes sense.

Three Steps You Can Take to Be a Social Entrepreneur

What can a small business owner do to become a social entrepreneur? Following are some steps that every business can take to head in the direction of social entrepreneurship.

1. Go Green Even if you're a home-based CEO, there are simple steps you can take to help the environment—the easiest and most obvious of which is to recycle. Nearly every city has some sort of recycling program for your paper, cardboard, glass, and metal waste; however, you can go a step further. Rather than throwing that draft print job in the recycling bin, why not use it as scratch paper, and then toss it to the recyclers once it's *really* used up? Also consider printing noncritical documents on the other side of already-used pages. This not only makes sense from an environmental standpoint, but it also ends up saving money as you won't use as much new paper.

Make some small changes as well, like switching to more energy efficient light bulbs, turning off unnecessary lights and equipment, and keeping your thermostat at a reasonable level. These steps can reduce your utility bills while conserving energy. Any new practice you undertake will help to make a difference—and those changes that save energy or reuse materials will add to your bottom line as well.

You can find another benefit of making some green changes to your company in the rebates, grants, and tax deductions offered by many states and state-regulated utility companies. Look into which programs are available in your state, and which federal benefits are currently being offered at the Database of State Incentives for Renewables & Efficiency (DSIRE). You can find the Web site in the resources section at the back of the book.

2. Give Stuff Away   Is it time to replace that old printer, copier, or PC? If so, don't just throw it out. If it still works or just needs some TLC, there are organizations in your community that can use it. Check out the National Christina Foundation or TechSoup Stock to find out how to donate your used electronics to a good cause. (We've included links to their sites in the Resources section.) If you have a company with several employees, consider holding food or clothing drives a couple of times a year. People are not just in need during the holidays, and local charities are always happy to take your donations. You'll feel great about giving, and the positive PR won't hurt any either.

3. Pick a Cause   As an entrepreneur, you know it's important to focus on what you're most passionate about. The same is true when it comes to doing good deeds. Pick a topic that appeals to you within the realm of social responsibility, and concentrate your efforts on making a difference in that area. Of course, if you choose to work on saving the rain forest, you'll still recycle and employ socially responsible business practices in other ways, but your primary focus might be on rain forest conservation efforts and the charities that support that. If it's the environment about which you're most concerned, you might aim to reduce your carbon footprint by 30 percent and attempt to go paperless within 12 months. If your heartstrings are pulled by undernourished children, you might donate 5 percent of your profits to a related charity, and sponsor a citywide food drive for them every year. Whatever cause you choose, know that your company will become linked to that cause if you do a good job of supporting it—which is something that your customers and potential customers see. So it's good for business, as well as good for the soul.

It's no secret that we all like to make money. But finding meaning and fulfillment in our lives is a universal need, and one many entrepreneurs hope to satisfy through starting a business. Becoming a socially responsible entrepreneur helps us to do both. When we're doing what we love, making money, *and* helping to make the world a better place to live, what more can anyone ask for?

Scott Harrison of charity: water—our next Entrepreneurial Profile—is a person who has taken his passion for a cause and done amazing things.

Entrepreneurial Profile: Scott Harrison
of charity: water

The drive, ambition, and entrepreneurial spirit that Scott Harrison exhibits leaves little doubt that he could have started any kind of business he wanted. In fact, after a 10-year foray into special event planning and promotions, Scott started an upscale event planning and nightclub consultancy, with clients including MTV, VH1, ABC, *Cosmopolitan*, *ELLE*, Xbox (Microsoft), Universal Records, RCA, Island Records, Dunkin Donuts, Bacardi USA, Nike, Anheuser-Busch, and more. However, he left the event business in August 2004 to serve for a year as a volunteer photojournalist onboard the Mercy Ship *Anastasis* in impoverished Liberia, West Africa. In September 2005, on returning home to New York City, Scott tested the idea behind charity: water by producing a large exhibition of his photographs and videos called *Mercy*. Although Scott's Mercy show opened in the midst of the Hurricane Katrina disaster, it was a success. Visitors contributed more than $96,000 toward providing medical procedures and freshwater wells in West Africa. Scott returned to West Africa for another six-month journey in October 2005, before returning to Manhattan in the spring of 2006 to found charity: water.

What led Scott in the direction of social entrepreneurship: "I left a decade of decadent living and a career in nightlife after coming back to my Christian faith at 28 years old, and I wanted to actually put action to it. I'd been living

(continued)

(continued)

selfishly, and only for me. It took me a little while, but I found an opportunity to serve as a volunteer photojournalist on a hospital ship in Liberia.

"I was prepared for small quarters, but not really expecting what I found. I first moved into a tiny 200-square-foot cabin with bunk beds that contained two roommates I'd never met, and cockroaches that loved coming up through the shower drain . . . it was clearly very different from my life and spacious apartment in New York City.

"However, when I ventured off the ship into the city and rural communities, I quickly realized how good I had it, and how much I had to be thankful for. At the time, Liberia had no public running water, sewage, or mail systems. It was a broken, brutally poor country after enduring 14 years of civil war. After being thrown into the midst of the extreme poverty there, I simply couldn't turn my back on it."

How Scott developed the concept for charity: water: "The idea came from the time I spent in Liberia. Although I was on a hospital ship that specialized in facial surgeries like tumor removal, cleft lip and palate correction, and burn treatment, they also ran a small water program that helped people in rural communities get clean water through the digging of shallow wells. As I traveled to the villages with the program director, I just couldn't believe the sources of water people were using—green, scum-filled ponds, dirty rivers. We looked at each other several times and said, 'Well, no wonder everyone around here is sick. . . . No wonder we're seeing so much disease.'

"I later learned that a billion people around the world lacked this most basic need, and that nobody had really stepped up to meet their great needs in this area. When I knew what we'd focus on, I looked around at the nonprofit sector, and realized I didn't want my organization to look anything like the norm. I wanted to reinvent charity. I had the faith that we could make a 100 percent donation model work and find a way to sustain it as we scaled. I believed that we could build an epic brand on a foundation of integrity and excellence, and then show people where their money went and the impact their gifts really had."

Scott's advice for entrepreneurs interested in taking the path of a social entrepreneur: "I guess I'm on the extreme end of the social entrepreneur scale, as our organization gives away literally 100 percent of the money we generate from the public. You can't be obsessed with money. So many people worship money and chase the big liquidity moment. You have to believe in your mission, your people, and the organization. And most importantly, you need to be sold on the social impact you're considering. In my case, bringing clean water to people in need around the world was a pretty easy sell."

Scott's advice for entrepreneurs interested in starting any business from the ground up: "Sit down and figure out the cost first. Then muster all the tenacity you have, and go forward. Don't let anyone tell you it can't be done, because they are wrong. Refuse to be discouraged. Stay humble and know what you don't know. Make sure there is integrity in all you do. Build a group of advisors that hold

(continued)

(continued)

you accountable, and be honest with them. Make room for think time. Say you're sorry. Get a coach. Work your butt off."

How having a Big Vision has played a part in Scott's success: "Trying to solve a global problem as big as a billion people without water has certainly helped guide me personally. It's daunting, and hard to get your head around. When we helped our first million people, I realized that we'd only solved 1/1000th of a problem. But now we're closing in on 1/500th of the problem, and many others have also stepped up to do their part. Jim Collins talks about the concept of 'Big Fat Hairy Goals' in his book, *Good to Great.* I truly believe that had we not had such a big vision, we'd have had a fraction of the success that we've seen in the last few years."

How Scott defines success: "I try to keep my priorities straight and am always trying to find the right balance. For me, it's God first, family second, and then everything else, and then some goes into the work and mission."

8

Pulling a 180

The Business Turnaround

When you reach an obstacle, turn it into an opportunity. You have the choice. You can overcome and be a winner, or you can allow it to overcome you and be a loser. The choice is yours and yours alone. Refuse to throw in the towel. Go that extra mile that failures refuse to travel. It is far better to be exhausted from success than to be rested from failure.

—Mary Kay Ash, founder of Mary Kay Cosmetics

W e've talked about the one quality that separates entrepreneurs from everyone else: a willingness to take risks. Exactly what risk is involved in entrepreneurship? It's the fact that sometimes, despite all your best planning and efforts to make your business thrive, you can end up in trouble—on the brink of going out of business, and maybe even losing everything. It could be that you made a mistake in predicting your original idea's viability, or underestimated your capital needs. It might be that something completely unexpected happened, like the economy taking a nosedive—something we saw on a wide scale a few years ago. Consider the many homebuilders who were great businesspeople, had plenty of capital, and were soaring high for years prior to 2008—and then lost it all when the market went away virtually overnight. Some might say they should have seen it coming, but hindsight is always 20/20, and not many people predicted what ended up happening.

Company failures don't always require a major event—like the housing crisis of 2008—to take place. Markets change, new technologies emerge and replace others, trends come and go, and additional competitors seem to spring from out of the blue on a continual basis. Things that we can't always see coming take place—and can sink our businesses if we're not ready for them.

So how can you possibly prepare for something you can't predict? And how can you "pull a 180" when it happens? It's obviously impossible to be ready for every contingency that you could ever confront; at least, it is not possible to predict every *specific* contingency. On the other hand, it *is* possible to cultivate a company culture and attitude that is able to effectively handle just about anything that comes your way. You can prepare for unexpected changes and obstacles if you simply embrace an important concept that we have stressed throughout this book: Flexibility.

Flexibility Allows for Transformation

There is a phrase we've all heard that can be a killer of companies. It is spoken in the corporate world more often than in small business, and although an employee is more likely to utter it than an entrepreneur, we've heard similar sentiments from many business owners as well. Someone usually uses this phrase after being asked to explain why a particular policy, procedure, or process is the standard for a given situation. The response that often comes is, *"Because that's how we've always done it."*

If there was a way to banish that phrase from the English language, we would be all for it. It isn't just a group of harmless words, the worst possible explanation for anything, and the worst reason for doing anything. It reflects a lack of creativity, an attitude of laziness, and a serious absence of flexibility. It's a company killer because it is anything but progressive, and you can bet that at least one of your competitors refuses to look at things that way.

Staying competitive—not to mention alive—in today's fast-paced, rapidly changing business environment demands that a company remain nimble and ready to head in a new direction at any moment. The world of business, including technology, marketing, buying trends, and customer expectations, are in constant flux. Unless business owners are ready and willing to adapt when it makes sense to do so—and *as soon as* it makes sense to do so—they risk losing in a big way. How many companies that went under during the economic downturn could have made it through had they been more nimble and willing to adapt on the fly? Although we may never know, it's a good bet that some that didn't make it were so entrenched in the way they "had always done things" that they weren't able to make the necessary adjustments to meet the challenges they didn't see coming.

So how do you alter this attitude if it's part of your business? The first step is to eliminate the belief that change is a bad thing. Although it can be inconvenient and accompanied by certain challenges, those events that might even seem negative can often end up providing a huge opportunity. And because change is inevitable in *any* industry, resisting it is both futile and counterproductive. It is better to anticipate and adapt as necessary by accepting reality and making the most of it.

To that end, the following are three essential keys for embracing change and remaining flexible:

1. **Avoid isolation.** As entrepreneurs, we can sometimes get so wrapped up in our businesses we end up inadvertently putting blinders on to everything else that's going on in the world. Make sure that you're getting out and spending time among colleagues, customers, industry leaders, and others who can clue you in on your industry's—and business in general's—recent events and developments.

    Your goal should be to have your finger on the pulse of both your industry and the general economic climate *at all times.* You want to see trends and changes coming from a mile away. Not only will this help you anticipate and respond to changes quickly and effectively; you might just find yourself becoming a leader in your field.

    "Getting out there" means spending time online as much as out in the community. Attending networking events, industry conventions, and other business gatherings is a great way to rub shoulders with fellow business leaders, and we wholly recommend participating in these activities. However, you don't always have to leave your office to realize many of the same benefits that these events present to you. Social media, industry forums and blogs, and trade association Web sites provide you with an opportunity to meet and interact with others in your industry to discuss current trends and best practices. Devote a half hour each day to checking in on the sites you find valuable, and get to know those who are the most informative about the state of your industry and business in general.

2. **Cultivate a culture of ingenuity.** Companies that are the most prepared to adapt to change are those where everyone, from the CEO down, embraces ingenuity. If you encourage your people to think about how to do things better, you'll be surprised at what they produce. So many times, employees, partners, and even contractors have great ideas that they never voice—simply because no one ever asked them, or they felt as though their opinions didn't matter. If you let people know that you will—even *want* to—hear and consider their suggestions and ideas, you'll get valuable feedback that can make a huge difference in your business.

Moreover, encouraging this kind of culture within your company will make people more adaptable to and accepting of change. When something happens that requires you to alter the way you do something—or even if you have to completely reinvent your company—your team will be more prepared to roll with the changes. Not only is this kind of culture conducive to long-term success, it can also be a lot of fun!

3. **Form mastermind groups within your company.** A mastermind group is usually made up of 5 to 10 people who

come together to discuss a specific topic, or just for general brainstorming purposes. You can use mastermind groups as internal focus groups to provide feedback on marketing campaigns; to help solve specific product or customer issues; or to present ideas for transitioning into a new direction.

This idea supports your atmosphere of ingenuity and takes it one step further. It shows that you aren't merely open to change and ideas; additionally, you can use these mastermind groups to proactively think of ways to improve existing processes and policies. These groups should be comprised of a wide range of positions with your organization, from management to entry level, and must include people who interact with your customers on a regular basis.

Even if you're a solopreneur, the overall objective of creating an attitude of flexibility is the same. Get feedback from people from both within and outside your company on a regular basis; remain open to change and new ideas; and regularly review how you do things, while always looking for new and better methods. You'll keep your company at the top of its game by remaining adaptable. This way, when the unexpected occurs, you'll be better prepared to take on and even make the most of the challenge.

So what does all this flexibility and embracing change lead to? It can ultimately mean your very survival as a company. When something that could otherwise be a catastrophic event comes your way, your company will be more able to adapt and move in the direction of the change, rather than fighting a losing battle against it. We've stressed vision a lot in this book, and one thing we have learned from the hundreds of entrepreneurs with whom we've talked over the years is that their initial vision for their company almost *never* matches where their company is today. In some cases, their companies are different in almost every way compared to their original concept. Without flexibility and an attitude of ingenuity, many of these businesses would have folded. But they were able to reinvent themselves because they focused more intently on the way things would work *best*—rather than "the way things have always been done."

One entrepreneur who has learned how to embrace change and remain flexible is Matt Mickiewicz, the subject of our next Entrepreneurial Profile.

Entrepreneurial Profile: Matt Mickiewicz of SitePoint and 99designs

Matt Mickiewicz launched Webmaster-Resources.com (which later became SitePoint) on April 1, 1998, with $100 of allowance money from his parents while he was still in high school. By age 16, Matt was driving a BMW he had paid for with cash. A few years later, he became the youngest house buyer (without a co-signer) in British Columbia's history—two weeks after his 19th birthday.

Today, Matt is the co-founder of SitePoint, the number-one Internet destination for Web professionals. The company was named one of the 100 fastest-growing businesses among all categories by *BRW Magazine* for three years in a row, and has appeared on the Delloite & Touche Technology Fast 50 numerous times. In February 2008, Matt co-founded 99designs—the largest crowdsourcing marketplace for graphic design—and followed it up with the launch of his third company, Flippa.com in June 2009. All three companies are profitable and turning over eight figures annually (combined).

Matt's "pulling a 180" story: "Like many media companies in 1999/2000, we built our entire business model around driving page views and making advertising sales. This wasn't a problem when all the rich, venture-backed Silicon Valley companies were calling us daily and begging to give us their marketing dollars; however, things changed quickly when the NASDAQ bubble imploded. At that point, we had employees, an office, and my business partner had quit his regular day job; failure was simply not an option.

(*continued*)

(*continued*)

"We had a look at what people were doing on SitePoint.com, and one of the most popular links on any given page was the 'Print This Article' link. It made sense; back then, no one had two monitors on their desktop. Therefore, they preferred to have the printed content sitting next to their keyboard to follow along when they were learning to code.

"So we had a thesis, and needed a quick and cheap way to find out whether it was right. We took our most popular tutorial about PHP and MySQL, and turned it into a print-on-demand book in a few weeks time (no inventory risk, and outsourced fulfillment). Despite making the content available for free online, thousands of people shelled out $35 to purchase a hardcopy of the book—and we were off to the races!"

How Matt and his team used reinvention to start 99designs.com: "One of the most popular sections of the SitePoint forums in 2006 was our Design Contests Forum. This initiative allowed Web site owners to post a discussion thread requesting design work along with their budget. Designers would then respond with fully completed design concepts. Typically, several dozen designers responded, giving the Web site owners the opportunity to choose from among dozens of submissions and only pay for the one they liked the best.

"While using Forum software to run a 'Design Contest' was awkward and fraught with perils, it seemed that both designers and site owners got tremendous value out of the offering. After building some basic software in six weeks time to smooth the process, and doubling our fee structure in 2007, we continued to see massive month over month growth. What surprised us the most, though, were the types of companies getting design work done, because all of a sudden, it wasn't just bloggers and Web site owners anymore. We had spas, dentists, realtors, and coffee shop owners visiting SitePoint.com to get stuff designed.

"We knew based on the book *The 22 Immutable Laws of Branding* [Al Ries and Laura Ries, HarperCollins, 1998] that the quickest way to destroy a brand was to have it stand for everything. SitePoint was about education for developers and designers, not graphic design outsourcing. So, we began work on 99designs, and eventually launched in February of 2008 with another 100 percent price increase. The new, memorable brand and simplified interface prompted growth to skyrocket—and massive publicity to follow. We had single-handedly disrupted the $12 billion graphic design industry, helped spur dozens of copycat competitors, and built an eight-figure business that went on to win a 2010 Webby Award for Best Web Service— beating out industry leaders DropBox and Tumblr."

Matt stresses the importance of remaining flexible in your business plans and structure: "If you had told me back in 1998 that we'd be publishing books, running a crowdsourcing marketplace for graphic design, and doing Web site auctions, I would have thought you were crazy. We achieved our two big successes by being able to shift from advertising to book sales on SitePoint. We then leveraged the SitePoint audience, distribution, and readers' natural tendencies to want to do business with each other to create two new spin-off companies. Additionally, the

(continued)

(continued)

massive amount of traffic we already had gave us a huge advantage over competitors."

Matt's advice for entrepreneurs interested in starting a company from the ground up: "Being able to deal with ambiguity and uncertainty and still make decisions to move forward is key to success, along with an intensive focus on customer service. Make sure you're willing to do whatever it takes, for as long as it takes to make your company a success—because I guarantee that it will take much longer than you ever thought. Start charging early, even when your product isn't flawless. It's better to get something out early and get market feedback than spend a year 'perfecting' something that no one cares about or wants to buy. Finally, practice frugality. Barter wherever possible, and never be afraid to ask for a discount, better payment terms, or additional value-add from anyone with whom you're spending money."

How having a Big Vision has played a part in Matt's success: "My business partner, Mark Harbottle and I, have always been focused on delivering maximum value to the end user, and not necessarily grabbing every last penny on the table for ourselves. Flippa.com has allowed us to help people sell over $50,000,000 worth of Web sites and create liquidity where none existed before. At 99designs, we've helped tens of thousands of up-and-coming designers find new clients, improve their skills, and earn extra money. And with SitePoint, we've empowered hundreds of thousands of people to get ahead in their entrepreneurial pursuits and careers by teaching them about PHP, MySQL, CSS, and other Web technologies. It's immensely gratifying to hear from our customers who succeeded—at least in some small part—because of the information, tools, or services that we provided them."

How Matt defines success: "Success is the absolute freedom and responsibility that comes from being your own boss."

What to Do Before You Give Up

You understand the importance of remaining flexible and nimble as a company; you make an effort to stay current on trends to anticipate challenges; and you know how to embrace and make the most of change. Is all that a guarantee of success? No, of course not. Unfortunately, there are no guarantees in business, and you can still find yourself on the brink of failure even after doing everything right. Though the possibility of failing isn't a reality anyone likes to contemplate—and is something we all wish was not an option—it happens. In fact, depending on which statistics you read, companies fail from just less than half the time to most of the time.

By following the advice we've provided throughout this book, you will dramatically decrease your chances of falling within the failure statistics. But what do you do when nothing else has worked? How do you know when to keep striving, and when to call it quits? This is ultimately a personal decision. But based on our experience with turning around several companies on our own and coaching many entrepreneurs to do the same for their businesses, we have some advice on what to do before you decide to throw in the towel.

Four Steps to Take Before You Give Up

If you're struggling in your business and don't know what else to try, start with the following four steps. Not only can these steps help to save your business, but they'll help you come out the other end stronger than ever.

1. Reevaluate *Everything*   Another phrase of the American English vernacular that we don't like is, "If it ain't broke, don't fix it." Much like, "That's how we've always done it," this phrase is limiting and unimaginative. It's the same as saying, "We're going to keep doing things the same way we always have and not consider the possibility that there might be a better way." But just because something seems to be working well doesn't mean it's working as well as it possibly *could*. When you're faced with the possibility of your business closing, it's time to re-evaluate everything you do from every imaginable angle. It might even help to look at your company as though you are considering starting it today. Some of the areas to assess include:

- **Your customers.** Talk with them to find out what you can do better. We're not talking about a comment card on the counter here; have genuine, back-and-forth conversations with them. Form a focus group made up of a cross section of your customers. Include some of the best, some occasional customers, and even some you've lost. It won't cost you any more than maybe a lunch for the group, and if you structure it right and ask the right questions, you'll receive invaluable feedback. Make sure you have a thick skin and approach this process determined to learn and act upon whatever comments you hear.

- **Your competition.** When you were thinking of starting your business, you looked at your competition to find out who they were, what they did well, and where you had opportunities to hold a competitive advantage. Continuous, ongoing competitive analysis is important—especially when things aren't going well. Have your competitors adapted to changes in the market better than you have? If so, why? How can you do things better or copy what they're doing? Remember, we're talking about your survival. It's time to swallow your pride and learn from whomever you can, even if it means admitting that your competitor might be doing things better than you are.

- **Your suppliers.** It's necessary to take a hard look at your vendors and the pricing you're getting across the board if you hope to do a 180. Far too many companies get in the habit of ordering from the same suppliers and fail to check whether their pricing is still competitive. Many organizations also develop strong relationships with suppliers over time, and sometimes even form friendships. This can make it difficult to look around for better pricing, terms, or other accommodations you might not currently be getting. However, if you go out of business, they're going to lose you as a client anyway, so why not evaluate all your vendor relationships and get bids on everything? Although it's fine to give your current suppliers a chance to match a lower bid, this is no time to keep doing business with a vendor who can't help you win your fight to save your company.

- **Your staff.** Your employees can be a great source of ideas for improving business, so be sure to tap them for their input. And just as with suppliers, it's not smart to keep people around who aren't significantly contributing to the cause when you're trying to turn your business around. Cutting or replacing employees can be one of the hardest things an entrepreneur has to do; but again, they'll be unemployed anyway if your company closes its doors. This is especially important when it comes to sales staff. You need to make sure that they are pulling their weight and bringing in quality sales. If they have discounting discretion, evaluate how they're using it, and make adjustments as necessary.

- **Your systems and processes.** Look at how you do all you do and figure out where you can streamline, and/or save time or money. Try to evaluate your operations with fresh eyes and see how you can improve everything you and your staff do each day. This is another area where your employees can be helpful. Ask for suggestions, and even consider rewarding their money-saving ideas with bonuses. It's a small price to pay if it allows you to save significantly over time.

2. Hire a Virtual Assistant   You might think that this sounds a little crazy, considering your business isn't doing well, but here's why it makes sense: as discussed in an earlier chapter, a virtual assistant (VA) can end up saving you a tremendous amount of time and money. The biggest advantage that a VA provides an entrepreneur with a struggling business is freeing you up to do what you do best—which is hopefully at the core of your business. No one will sell what you sell as well as you do, and no one will treat your customers like the owner of the company will. You're clearly not optimizing your time if you're stuck in your office figuring out payroll or responding to e-mail—and your company is likely suffering for it. Hire a VA, hand over as much as you can to them, and get back to running your business.

3. Network, Network, Network   You probably don't want to spend much time away from your business if it's floundering; however, it's important to do some strategic networking. Get out into your business community and start talking with other businesspeople. You never know where you'll find your next opportunity, big client, or breakthrough idea. Someone you meet at a networking event might be the ally you need to support you and provide you with ideas, information, or inspiration to keep your business alive.

Check out Meetup.com and search for networking events that are specific to your industry or that sound like they will be attended by people who could be clients or colleagues. Your local chamber of commerce probably puts on networking events at least once a month as well. We recommend steering clear of "mixer" events held at bars, as these often have a loud atmosphere that is not conducive to making professional connections. At the least, networking should surround you with people of like minds—and we can all use the energy that creates.

4. Bring in an Expert   If you've tried all you can and just aren't making the progress you would like, consider hiring a turnaround consultant. As some of the steps above illuminate, a big part of pulling a 180 is being able to look at things with a fresh pair of eyes. Turnaround experts provide that pair of eyes and then make recommendations to help you get things moving in the right direction. They will also be honest with you and let you know if a 180 just isn't in the cards. We've provided some links to a couple of great consultants in the Resources section toward the back of the book.

Pulling a 180 for your faltering company is by no means easy. It takes a lot of work, and there is no 100 percent guarantee that anything you do will work. That said—it is well worth the effort. If you are able to save your company, you will emerge stronger than ever before and better prepared for future challenges. You'll have streamlined processes in place, a fresh focus, and a lean operation. If the worst case scenario occurs and you have to close your business, you'll be able to say you did all you could, and you'll end up wiser and better prepared for the next opportunity that comes your way. You will also be in great company. Many of the most successful entrepreneurs in history failed time and again before finding success. The key is to get up and try again. After all, what else can a true entrepreneur do?

Mike Michalowicz, our next Entrepreneurial Profile, knows a lot about the ups and downs of turning a business around. His insights are valuable, so take notes!

Entrepreneurial Profile: Mike Michalowicz
of *The Toilet Paper Entrepreneur*

You might know Mike Michalowicz as a frequent guest of CNBCs *The Big Idea* with Donny Deutsch, ABC News, Fox News, or other television programs, or you might have read features about him in *Entrepreneur, Forbes, US News & World Report*, the *New York Times*, or other publications. Mike launched his first business at the age of 24, moving his young family to the only safe place he could afford—a retirement village. With limited resources and no experience, he systematically bootstrapped a multimillion-dollar technology business, while sleeping in conference rooms to avoid hotel costs. After selling his first company, Mike launched a new business the next day, and in less than three years, sold it to a Fortune 500 company.

Nowadays, Mike is known for his Web site, The Toilet Paper Entrepreneur, and his book by the same title. Mike knows what it takes for a business to pull a 180. As he puts it, "The Toilet Paper Entrepreneur's 'get real,' actionable approach to business is a much-needed swift kick in the pants." Additionally, his newest multimillion-dollar venture Obsidian Launch grows authors and experts into industry superstars.

How Mike can tell a business needs to pull a 180: "From my experience there is one big—better said, *huge*—indicator that something is not working: A lack of recurring customers. You have to understand that customers lie through their teeth, but speak the truth through their wallets. So it's not enough if a customer claims to 'love'

(continued)

(*continued*)

your product or promises to use your service; they are effectively 'lying' to you. They often express thoughts like these simply to be nice. However, when it comes to paying you for your product or service, the whole story can change. Now they need to talk to other people, or 'think about it.' Basically, the real truth is revealed when money becomes part of the conversation.

"If they pay you, they are saying loud and clear that they see value in what you have to offer. And if they pay you again and again—or buy from you repeatedly—they are saying that your service or your product is delivering its value.

"So, if you have spent enough time in your business that you technically should have recurring purchases from clients, but you don't—then it's time to throw in the towel. Or better yet, invent the next, better version of what you are doing."

Mike's number one step for pulling a 180: "Interview clients like mad. The funny thing is most entrepreneurs simply evaluate themselves critically. But the problem is the feedback you get from you talking to yourself is taken from the wrong perspective. So, if you want to do a true 180, sit down with your past clients or even people who decided to buy elsewhere. Tell them you have nothing to sell them; you simply want to improve your organization and change what you do. Therefore, you want their feedback on the bad and the ugly, and want to know their thoughts on how to improve or change your business."

Mike's take on turnaround experts: "Turnaround experts are a great idea—but not for the reason many people think. They don't come in with a magic formula or pixie dust, but they do come in with a different vantage point. When you bring in an outsider, you introduce different experiences, a different view, and potentially different ideas.

"The key is to structure their involvement where they win only if they turn around your company. You want everyone's skin in the game—both theirs and yours. This will ensure that everyone is working on the same goal: fixing the company. Often, the best way to do this is to give them a piece of equity, or define clear performance metrics that they must achieve for them to be compensated."

Mike's advice for entrepreneurs interested in starting a company from the ground up: "First you must know that *passion does* not *guarantee success.* But ironically, you *will* be best served by doing what you are passionate about. Here is the whole trick: Passion brings about persistence and the tendency to stick-to-it, and that determination is ultimately what brings about success.

"So I encourage any new entrepreneur to start a new business in a field they are passionate about—then stay with it. Listen to the customers (or lack thereof) and adjust. Find what is working and amplify it; discover what is not working and stop doing it. Systemize everything. Never stop. And then, just then, you might have a shot."

(*continued*)

(*continued*)

How having a Big Vision has played a part in Mike's success: "Having a Big Vision is always critical—and the reason it's so important is because it forces you to think differently, and through better questions. Instead of constantly asking myself, 'Why is this *not* working?'—which frequently results in useless answers—a big vision forces me to ask better questions. 'How do I make my big vision come true considering these circumstances?' Along with better questions come better answers—and better answers, when executed, bring the best results."

How Mike defines success: "The word *successful* is a totally loaded word, and we all have our definition. For me, to be successful is to:

1. Define clear goals for myself.
2. Meet them (or modify the goals if other factors make a variation of the goal look better).
3. Set new goals once I've achieved prior goals.

"For example, I felt successful when I got my driver's license as a teenager. But now a driver's license is far from successful for me and most other people; it is just the norm. Now the goal may be to acquire a car I admire, or perhaps to learn new driving skills (like defensive driving skills).

"The thing is that being successful is a very personal—in fact, exclusive—definition. We all define what success is for ourselves, and it changes over time. Success does not need to be a tangible thing. For example, while income level seems to be the most common published form of how people measure success, this is not always the case. It could be for some, or it might be part of it for some . . . but money isn't the only thing, and I don't even think it is the most important thing.

"One final thought: I think the definition of success can become a trap, too, if we define it by comparing our position to where we believe someone else is. To look at the other guy and say he has more money or more happiness or more whatever—and to believe that this means that he is more successful, and that I, by default, am *less* successful—is a trap. Success ultimately means identifying our own path, and then making it happen."

Afterword

Life is not made up of the haves and have-nots. Life is made up of the wills and will-nots.

—Larry Winget, author, speaker

Within the pages of this book, we've provided useful, practical information about how to start and run a small business, from the planning stages through expanding and marketing both your company and yourself. We've given you examples of entrepreneurs who have used these same methods to thrive in their own companies, and we've shared techniques for maintaining your vision and turning things around when the going gets tough.

We encourage you to return to the pages of this book often. Different chapters can have unique relevance at various points in your entrepreneurial journey; therefore, you can refer to the information we've provided in the chapters, as well as in the Resources section, time and again as needed. If you're looking for a boost of encouragement, reread Chapter 1 on having a big vision. If your marketing is stalled and you want to bring more traffic to your Web site or through your door, turn to Chapter 5 on laser-sighted marketing. And you can always refer to any of the entrepreneurial profiles to reinforce the fact that you can do anything you put your mind to.

Of course, reading a book—any book—won't mean a thing unless you put the advice contained within it into practice. We can give you all the ingredients of success we're able to supply, but the most important element must come from within you. You'll only be successful as an entrepreneur when you take the necessary actions and decide that you're going to do whatever it takes to achieve success. The will and fortitude to take those actions cannot come from anyone but you.

As an entrepreneur, you already know that. Entrepreneurs are the achievers of the world. We're the ones who take action while others are content to sit on the sidelines. We don't just complain about the way things are when times are hard; we get off our butts and *do* something about it. We see problems as opportunities for solutions, and failures as chances to learn. That's why presidents call on entrepreneurs in hard economic times and often include help to small business owners as part of recovery packages. Presidents know that even when things are looking most grim, small business owners—and those who are brave and resourceful enough to start new businesses—will not sit by and let everything fall apart. Entrepreneurs put people back to work and bring value to their communities. We find ways to innovate and move forward, no matter the odds.

The term *entrepreneurial spirit* describes something beyond tendencies or preferences. It refers to a deep, unstoppable need to create and build, to accomplish, and to succeed. Entrepreneurial spirit is what fuels our creativity and passion, and what keeps us going when our backs are against the wall. The strength of your entrepreneurial spirit might ebb and flow; however, it is a reliable constant in true entrepreneurs' lives. Everyone has doubts from time to time, and our feelings of discouragement can sometimes knock us down. Yet the difference between true entrepreneurs and everyone else is that while we may be down, we are never *out*. What would equal a deathblow to many only serves to fuel our success. We know that failure is simply not an option.

Throughout this book and in countless interviews for our Web sites, we have profiled successful entrepreneurs from a wide range of industries and backgrounds. You will find that in most ways, they are no different from anyone else. The only dissimilarity is that they have taken the action necessary to guarantee their own success. This action isn't some secret ritual or rite that is known to a select few. The actions that make entrepreneurs successful are simply the ones that move them—however slightly and gradually—toward their goals. You've heard us say it over and over again—it all comes down to passion and vision.

So our final advice to you is to keep going, and never ever, ever give up. Keep working toward your *Big Vision*, and don't let anyone or anything stand in your way. What terrifies you most should not be the thought of failure; it should be thought of quitting just before the breakthrough that would have meant your ultimate success. So when you come up against challenges and obstacles (and you will), let your vision be your guide and your passion be the force that drives you. Success is waiting for you on the other side!

Resources

Stay in Touch with Us
- Web site for this book
  www.SmallBusinessBigVision.com
- Follow us on Twitter (@thebizguy)
  http://twitter.com/thebizguy
- Find us on Facebook
  www.facebook.com/YoungEntrepreneurs
- Young Entrepreneur Web site
  www.YoungEntrepreneur.com
- Blogtrepreneur Web site
  www.Blogtrepreneur.com
- SelfMade Web site
  www.SelfMade.net
- Kidpreneurs
  www.Kidpreneurs.org

Stay in Touch with Entrepreneurs Featured in This Book
- Dan Schawbel
  http://DanSchawbel.com

www.PersonalBrandingBlog.com

http://twitter.com/DanSchawbel

- David Hauser and Siamak Taghaddos

  http://GrasshopperGroup.com

  http://twitter.com/ghgroup

  http://DavidHauser.com

- Brent Oxley

  www.HostGator.com

  http://twitter.com/HostGator

- Brock Blake

  www.FundingUniverse.com

  http://BrockBlake.com

  http://twitter.com/FundingUniverse

- Gabriel Shaoolian

  www.BlueFountainMedia.com

  http://twitter.com/BFMWeb

- Anita Campbell

  http://SmallBizTrends.com

  www.BizSugar.com

  http://twitter.com/SmallBizTrends

- Ali Brown

  www.AliBrown.com

  www.TheAliMagazine.com

  http://twitter.com/AliBrownla

- Daven Michaels

  www.123Employee.com

http://DavenMichaels.com/

http://twitter.com/DavenMichaels

- Gary Vaynerchuk

http://GaryVaynerchuk.com

http://WineLibrary.com

http://twitter.com/garyvee

- Mike Roberts

www.SpyFu.com

http://twitter.com/mrspy

- Shama Hyder Kabani

www.MarketingZen.com

http://shama.tv

http://twitter.com/shama

- Adam Braun

www.PencilsofPromise.org

http://twitter.com/itsAdamBraun

- Scott Harrison

www.charitywater.org

http://twitter.com/ScottHarrison

- Matt Mickiewicz

www.SitePoint.com

http://99designs.com

http://twitter.com/sitepointmatt

- Mike Michalowicz

www.ToiletPaperEntrepreneur.com

http://twitter.com/tpentrepreneur

Awesome Tools for Today's Entrepreneurs

Billing and Accounting
- FreshBooks
  www.FreshBooks.com
- Kashoo
  www.Kashoo.com

Business Networking
- Chamber of Commerce Directory
  www.ChamberofCommerce.com/chambers
- Meetup
  www.Meetup.com

Business Plan Help
- Business Plan Pro template software
  www.PaloAlto.com/business_plan_software
- Free Excel Spreadsheets for financial projections, and others
  www.exinfm.com/free_spreadsheets.html
- Growthink's Ultimate Business Plan Template
  www.GrowThink.com/products/business-plan-template

Business Turnaround Consultants
- ActionCOACH
  http://ActionCOACH.com
- Dorset Partners
  www.DorsetPartners.com

Collaboration Tools

- Basecamp
  http://Basecamphq.com
- OfficeMedium
  www.OfficeMedium.com

Customer Relationship Management

- Salesforce
  www.Salesforce.com/
- Zoho CRM
  www.Zoho.com/crm

E-Commerce

- ClickBank
  www.ClickBank.com
- MySiteSales.com
  http://MySiteSales.com

File Storage and Backup

- BackupElf
  http://BackupElf.com
- Dropbox
  www.Dropbox.com

Finding Niches

- Ask500People.com
  www.Ask500People.com
- 43Things
  www.43Things.com

Group and Team Communication

- HipChat

  www.HipChat.com

- Yammer

  www.Yammer.com

Legal

- LegalZoom

  www.LegalZoom.com

- Nolo

  www.Nolo.com

Money Management

- Mint

  www.Mint.com

- SmartyPig

  www.SmartyPig.com

Personal Branding

- Experts Academy

  www.ExpertsAcademy.com

- Personal Branding Blog

  www.PersonalBrandingBlog.com

Press Releases

- PitchEngine

  www.PitchEngine.com

- PRWeb

  www.PRWeb.com

Productivity Tools

- Jott Assistant (Voice-to-text notes)
  http://Jott.com/jott/jott-assistant.html
- PortableApps.com
  http://PortableApps.com

Social Entrepreneurship Resources

- Database of State Incentives for Renewables
  and Efficiency
  www.dsireusa.org
- National Christina Foundation (donate used equipment)
  www.Cristina.org
- Tech Soup Stock (technology donations)
  www.TechSoup.org/stock

Social Media Tools

- Hootsuite
  www.Hootsuite.com
- TweetDeck
  www.TweetDeck.com

Virtual Assistants and Outsourcing

- 123Employee
  www.123Employee.com
- Elance
  www.Elance.com
- Guru
  www.Guru.com

- Virtual Zeta
  www.VirtualZeta.com

Web site Optimization

- SEOmoz
  www.SEOmoz.org
- SEOToolSet
  www.SEOtoolSet.com

Epigraph Sources

Chapter 1

Tichy, Noel, and Charan, Ram. "Speed, Simplicity, and Self-Confidence." *Harvard Business Review* (September–October 1989).

Chapter 2

Butcher, Mike. "TC50: Angel Investors Say Now Is Their Time." Tech Crunch (2008). http://techcrunch.com/2008/09/08/tc50-angel-investors-say-now-is-their-time/.

Chapter 3

Anderson, Anthony. "A Time for Adaptation." *Huffington Post* (2009). www.huffingtonpost.com/anthony-anderson/a-time-for-adaptation_b_170948.html.

Chapter 4

Buckman, John. "Employees Suck. Don't Be One. Don't Hire One." Speech given at LeWeb 2008, Paris.

Chapter 5

Mitch, Joel. *Six Pixels of Separation*. New York: Hachette, 2009.

Chapter 6

Godin, Seth. *Small Is the New Big*. New York: Penguin, 2006.

Chapter 7

Kawasaki, Guy. *The Art of the Start*. London: Portfolio, 2004.

Chapter 8

Ash, Mary Kay. "Mary Kay Quotes on Success." Mary Kay Tribute: Celebrating Mary Kay Ash, www.marykaytribute.com/WisdomSuccess .aspx, Unk (accessed January 25, 2011).

Afterword

Winget, Larry. *People Are Idiots and I Can Prove It*. New York: Gotham Books, 2009.

Index